Alan Paton
Revised Edition

Twayne's World Authors Series

Bernth Lindfors, Editor of South African Literature

University of Texas at Austin

TWAS 40

ALAN PATON
(1903 –   )
Photograph by Crown Studios.
Reproduced with the permission
of Charles Scribner's Sons.

Alan Paton
Revised Edition

By Edward Callan

Twayne Publishers · Boston

Alan Paton, Revised Edition

Edward Callan

Copyright © 1982 by G. K. Hall & Company
All Rights Reserved
Published by Twayne Publishers
A Division of G. K. Hall & Company
70 Lincoln Street
Boston, Massachusetts 02111

Book Production by Marne B. Sultz
Book Design by Barbara Anderson

Printed on permanent/durable acid-free
paper and bound in the United States of
America.

Library of Congress Cataloging in Publication Data

Callan, Edward, 1917–
    Alan Paton.

    (Twayne's world authors series ;
TWAS 40)
    Bibliography: p. 135
    Includes index.
    1. Paton, Alan—
Criticism and interpretation.
I. Title. II. Series
PR9369.3.P37Z6   1982   823   82-11970
ISBN 0-8057-6512-3

Contents

About the Author

Edward Callan was born in Ireland and educated there as well as in England, South Africa, and the United States. He studied and taught in South Africa between 1937 and 1949, and served with the South African Field Artillery in North Africa and Italy in World War II. After the war he earned advanced degrees at South African and American universities and undertook postdoctoral study at St. Antony's College, Oxford University. He first met Alan Paton in 1948.

Dr. Callan came to the United States in 1952. He is professor of English at Western Michigan University, where he received the Distinguished Faculty Scholar Award in 1980. His recent books include *Carnival of Intellect: Auden and His Work* (Oxford University Press, 1982) and *Yeats on Yeats* (Dublin: The Dolmen Press, 1981). He has written essays on literature for many journals including *London Magazine, Dublin Magazine, Saturday Review, Commonweal, Southern Review, University of Toronto Quarterly, New York Times Book Review, The Times* (London), and *Research in African Literatures*.

Dr. Callan's writings on South African topics include the first monograph on the 1961 Nobel Peace Prize laureate, Chief Albert Luthuli, and an edition of Alan Paton's political writings: *The Long View* (1967), which also appeared in Swedish translation. In 1970 he compiled the volume *Alan Paton* in the German series "Hamburger Bibliographien" (ed. Rolf Itaaliander; tr. F. Weidner). His 1968 edition of this TWAS study received appreciative reviews in South African and Australian newspapers; and *Choice*, the journal of the American Association of College and University Libraries, selected it for its annual list: "Outstanding Academic Books, 1969."

Preface

Since his first novel, *Cry, the Beloved Country*, was published in New York in 1948, Alan Paton has been regarded throughout most of the world as a respected interpreter of South African life and society. Within South Africa, prior to 1948, he had gained a fine professional reputation for his creative approach to problems of penal reform; and later, after the introduction of the racial system of *apartheid*, he felt compelled to enter public life as an active leader of the Liberal party to promote the spirit of nonracial democracy and respect for civil rights in South Africa.

One aim of this book is to provide essential background on Alan Paton's life and times, based in part on his 1981 volume of autobiography, *Towards the Mountain*. A second aim is to describe and evaluate his literary achievement in fiction, drama, biography, and poetry up to and including his 1982 novel, *Ah, But Your Land Is Beautiful*. But it also seeks, where possible, to show the related significance of his writings on politics and religion, and of his leadership of the South African Liberal party from 1956 until it was proclaimed illegal in 1968 because its membership was open to all races.

The term *nonracial* as used in this book is derived from the program of the Liberal party and Alan Paton's writings on race relations. It implies that the system of rigidly classifying people in racial groups should be replaced by some common term for South Africans.

Page numbers in parentheses included in the text refer to the United States standard edition of the work under discussion. Where more precise identification seems necessary the following abbreviations appear with page numbers: *AA (Apartheid and the Archbishop)*; *CBC (Cry, the Beloved Country)*; *FYD (For You Departed*, published in London as *Kontakion for You Departed)*; *KD (Knocking on the Door))*; *LV (The Long View)*; *TLP (Too Late the Phalarope)*; *TM (Towards the Mountain)*. Variant titles are indicated as follows: D. indicates *Debbie Go Home*; T., *Tales from a Troubled Land*; H., *Hofmeyr*; S A.T., *South African Tragedy*.

Acknowledgment is due to Alan Paton for permission to quote

from his early writings in the *Natal University College Magazine*; from his writings in *Contact* included in *The Long View* (New York: Praeger, 1968), and from his *Hope for South Africa* (New York: Praeger, 1959). Acknowledgment is also due to him and to his wife, Anne, for hospitality at Kloof, Natal, and for friendly correspondence over several years; to Jonathan Paton of the University of the Witwatersrand for much valuable assistance; to Ruth Shirley Lundie of the University of Natal Library; to Reuben Musiker of Rhodes University Library; and to Dr. Quentin White, director of the South African Institute of Race Relations.

Acknowledgment is also due to Charles Scribner's Sons, New York, for permission to quote from *Cry, the Beloved Country*; *Too Late the Phalarope*; *Tales from a Troubled Land*; *A South African Tragedy: The Life and Times of Jan Hofmeyr*; *Apartheid and the Archbishop*; *For You Departed*; and *Towards the Mountain* by Alan Paton; and from *Sponono*, a play by Alan Paton and Krishna Shah; to Studs Terkel for permission to quote from "Four Interviews" in *Perspectives on Arts and Ideas* (1963); to Holt, Reinhart and Winston, New York, for use of extracts from my Introduction to *The Long View* by Alan Paton (New York, Praeger, 1968); and to Jonathan Cape, Ltd., London, for permission to quote from *Kontakion For You Departed* and *Too Late the Phalarope* by Alan Paton.

I also wish to acknowledge the assistance of a Faculty Research Fellowship from the Faculty Research Committee, Western Michigan University.

Edward Callan

Western Michigan University

Chronology

1938   Joins Centenary celebrations of the Great Trek.

1939   Volunteers for military duty in World War II; not eligible on grounds of essential occupation; becomes chairman of combined YMCA and Toc-H (Talbot House) War Services.

1942   Appointed to Anglican Diocesan Commission to report on the church and race in South Africa.

1943   Series of articles on crime, punishment, and penal reform commissioned by the *Forum*.

1944   Address to the National Social Welfare Conference (published as *The Non-European Offender*, 1945).

1946   Takes leave of absence to study penal and correctional institutions in Europe, the United States, and Canada. Begins *Cry, the Beloved Country* in Trondheim, Norway.

1948   *Cry, the Beloved Country* (New York). Addresses National Penal Reform League Conference (published as *Freedom as a Reformatory Instrument*). Nationalist party election victory introduces policy of *apartheid* in South Africa. Resigns Diepkloof Reformatory. Jan Hofmeyr dies.

1949   Receives Ainsfield-Wolf Award (U.S.) and London *Times* Special Book Award for *Cry, the Beloved Country*. Visits the United States for Broadway opening of *Lost in the Stars*. Begins work on the biography of Jan Hofmeyr.

1951   *South Africa Today*.

1952   Writes *Too Late the Phalarope* in England.

1953   Joins Liberal party of South Africa as vice-president.

1954   Tours the United States to write on race relations for *Colliers*. Hon. L.H.D., Yale. Addresses World Council of Churches meetings, Evanston, Illinois.

1955   Writes *The Land and People of South Africa* for high-school students in the United States and Britain.

1956   Elected chairman of the South African Liberal party.

Becomes trustee of Treason Trial Defence Fund (later Defence and Aid Fund). Visits New York for dramatized version of *Too Late the Phalarope* by Robert Yale Libott.

1958   *Hope for South Africa*; *The People Wept*. Becomes national president of the Liberal party. Attends All-African Church Conference in Nigeria. Begins his series "The Long View" in *Contact*. Diepkloof Reformatory closed down. Dr. Verwoerd new prime minister.

1959   Delivers Stafford Cripps Memorial Sermon in St. Paul's Cathedral, London; published as *The Christian Approach to Racial Problems in the Modern World*; *The Last Journey*, a play about Dr. Livingstone.

1960   State of Emergency declared in South Africa on March 30. *Charlestown Story*; *Mkhumbane (Village in the Gulley)*, libretto for a musical with music by Todd Matshikiza. Receives the Freedom Award for 1960 from Freedom House, New York. Passport withdrawn on return home.

1961   *Tales from a Troubled Land* (New York) and *Debbie Go Home* (London); Award from Free Academy of Art, Hamburg.

1962   Hon. L.H.D., Kenyon College; *Sponono* (with Krishna Shah) produced in Durban and Johannesburg.

1964   *Hofmeyr* published in Cape Town; Broadway production of *Sponono*.

1965   *South African Tragedy: The Life and Times of Jan Hofmeyr* (United States edition of *Hofmeyr*); *Sponono*, published in New York.

1966   Defence and Aid Fund banned. Dr. Hendrik Verwoerd, Prime Minister of South Africa, assassinated. Blathazar J. Vorster succeeds him.

1967   October, Dorrie Paton dies.

1968   *The Long View*, ed. Edward Callan. Nonracial Liberal party made illegal under terms of Prohibition of Interference Act. Hon. D.L.H., University of Natal.

1969 *For You Departed* (*Kontakion for You Departed* in British edition); founding editor of *Reality: A Journal of Liberal Opinion*; marries Anne Hopkins.

1970 Passport restored for research on biography of Geoffrey Clayton in England.

1971 Hon. L.H.D., Harvard University; Hon. D.D., Edinburgh University; Hon. L.H.D., Trent University, Ontario.

1973 *Apartheid and the Archbishop: The Life and Times of Geoffrey Clayton, Archbishop of Cape Town*; Chubb Fellow, Yale University; Pringle Award.

1975 *Knocking on the Door: Shorter Writings of Alan Paton*, ed. Colin Gardner. Hon. L.L.B., University of the Witwatersrand.

1977 Visiting lecturer, University of Michigan at Flint; Western Michigan University; Michigan State University. Hon. L.H.D., University of Michigan.

1980 *Towards the Mountain* (New York).

1981 *Towards the Mountain* (London); *Ah, But Your Land Is Beautiful*, first novel of a proposed trilogy.

Chapter One

The Evolution of a Nonracial South African

The Pilgrim Way

Alan Paton was born in South Africa on 11 January 1903 in what was then the separate British colony of Natal, which now forms part of the Republic of South Africa. But to the world at large his history as a literary man began forty-five years later with the publication in New York of his first novel, *Cry, the Beloved Country*. Published in February 1948, this novel was very well received throughout the world by critics and by the reading public alike; and it soon became one of the best-known novels of the era.

Rarely has a first novel by an unknown writer achieved such wide popularity or succeeded in retaining so large a measure of that popularity with the passage of time. It was adapted for the Broadway stage as the musical *Lost in the Stars*, by Maxwell Anderson and Kurt Weill, in 1949.[1] During the next year it was filmed, partly on location in South Africa, by Alexander Korda.[2] It was later adapted as a verse drama by Felicia Komai.[3] And it was soon translated into some twenty languages in Europe, Asia, and Africa—with the Spanish and Portuguese editions widely distributed in Latin America.[4] Twenty-five years later, in 1973, Paton revealed that the novel "continues to sell a six-figure total every year" (*KD*, 274).

Such literary success by a man of forty-five may provoke speculation about novels he might have written had he turned to creative literature earlier. Paton might indeed have written other novels—perhaps even good ones—for he already had a substantial reputation as a writer and a speaker in South Africa where he wrote for professional journals and, fairly frequently, for the *Forum*, a fortnightly journal of liberal opinion. From his college days on, he had written verse occasionally, and he had attempted, and discarded, two or three novels of white South African life set in the beautiful Natal countryside in the vicinity of Ixopo, near Pietermaritzburg, where he had his first teaching assignment, and to which he introduces us in the opening cadences of *Cry, the Beloved Country*: "There is a lovely road that runs from Ixopo into the hills. . . ." But it is part of the purpose of this account of his literary achievement to suggest that, notwithstanding his skill as a writer, Paton could not have produced the profound work that *Cry, the Beloved Country* unquestionably is, prior to the time he began work on it during a visit to Trondheim, Norway, during 1946. He might have written other books, but not this book.

In the period before 1935, when he led the relatively comfortable life of a white schoolmaster in Natal, Paton had been insulated—as were most South African whites of his class—from the realities of black African life that inform his first novel. But in the couse of the next decade, while principal of a reform school for black youths in Johannesburg, he experienced a process of maturing that transformed his outlook. The decisive elements in this remarkable process were four in number: his experience with delinquent black youth; his association with the South African Institute of Race Relations; his part in an Anglican diocesan commission to study his church's attitude to racial affairs; and, in the background, the Second World War, 1939—45, and the measureless suffering caused by Hitler's racial megalomania.

As the director of a reformatory institution and subsequently in active political life, Paton upheld an ideal of human freedom based on mutual trust and acceptance of personal responsibility. This view of freedom recognizes a man's need to surmount the limitations of ignorance, illiteracy, or inbred prejudice so that he may develop his inherent human capacities. As principal of a reformatory, Paton relied on increasing freedom as his main instrument of reform. A youth committed to the reformatory for habitual theft, for example, would be given training in a useful trade, and, at the same time, increasingly exposed to the temptation to steal or to run away. If this exposure to freedom and responsibility succeeded, then on release he would not be simply someone freed from the reformatory, but a free man who had overcome the habit of stealing and gained the capacity for independent self-support. Again, the South African Liberal party, which Paton led for more than a decade before it was made illegal in 1968, described its ideal not as integration of the races, but as a nonracial society, that is, a society whose members have freed themselves from inbred racial prejudices. Speaking of the bans and restrictions placed on many of its members before the Liberal party, too, was made illegal, Paton said "What so angered the State . . . was the way in which the Party translated its ideal into practice, and actually made of itself the living embodiment of the kind of society it believed in."[5]

All of Paton's writings, his novels, his short fiction, his biographies of Jan Hofmeyr and Archbishop Clayton, and his own autobiography *Towards the Mountain*, express this consistent concern for the freedom, dignity, and worth of individual human beings—a concern that is based, ultimately, on his Christian convictions. Conflict in his fiction, both within individual characters and in society at large, often derives from confrontation between the affirmative Spirit of Liberty and the prohibiting Spirit that Denies. This encounter leads to an intellectual or spiritual quest in which some characters venture out beyond the restraint of exclusive loyalty to a group, a nation, or a race, and seek to assume the responsibilities of shared humanity.

Typically, in all of his literary work, Paton shows us his vision of reality—his way of seeing the world—through an allegory of the Pilgrim Way: a difficult but rewarding journey out from the darkness of closed minds and limited horizons into the light. The exemplary characters in his works of fiction develop intellectually not through discovering some new ideology or set of beliefs, but by becoming increasingly aware of their individual responsibility for serving a cause greater than themselves, such as furthering the cause of justice.

In *Cry, the Beloved Country*, for example, this theme of the Pilgrim Way is developed in the "Private Essay on the Evolution of a South African" found among the papers of the murdered man, Arthur Jarvis. This essay commences: "It is hard to be born a South African. One can be born an Afrikaner, or an English-speaking South African, or a coloured man, or a Zulu." And it goes on to admit: "One can see, as I saw when I was a boy, the reserves of the Bantu people, and see nothing of what was happening there at all" (174). In Paton's later work, the biography *Hofmeyr*, this theme of liberation from inhibiting local custom recurs like a refrain: "Hofmeyr was a white South African with white South African fears and prejudices and irrationalities . . . feeling his way out of the bog into which he had been born" (*H.*, 307, *S.A.T.*, 241).

Other characters set out on the Pilgrim Way from a variety of starting points. The elder Jarvis in *Cry, the Beloved Country*, for example, begins to emerge gradually from the closed mental world of his habitual white South African assumptions as he seeks to understand the unprejudiced spirit that informed the life and actions of his son. Nor is the Pilgrim Way, like so much in South Africa, reserved for whites only. The old African pastor Stephen Kumalo also begins to emerge from the closed trap of unthinking acceptance when, on returning from Johannesburg, he seeks out the village chief and the schoolmaster and attempts to get them to take some initiative in grappling with immediate problems.

The same theme of pilgrimage informs *For You Departed*, Paton's memorial for his first wife, Dorrie. This work shows that the pilgrimage toward release from conventional white South African attitudes is undertaken gradually and fearfully. It traces the ascending path from "the halcyon days" of thoughtless acceptance of white South African privilege with its unreasoning pride in the sun, and the gold, and the generosity of nature. The pilgrim proceeds from this unexamined complacency to a growing sensitivity for human suffering, and, ultimately, to a willingness to suffer for what he believes in—as did many members of the Liberal party. And in the course of *For You Departed*, Paton himself speaks of *Cry, the Beloved Country* as an allegory of the Pilgrim Way—out from the privileged background of Natal farm life that Dorrie Paton had come from—when he says of that novel: "It is a song of love for one's far distant country, it is informed with longing for that land . . . where there shall be no more death, . . . for that land that cannot be again, of hills, and grass, and bracken, the land where you were born" (*FYD*, 88).

The Pilgrim Way begins in childhood innocence to which none can return in maturity; and it leads toward a terminus always out of reach. This terminus can be expressed in symbolic terms as an ideal to be worked for—like the Promised Land toward which Moses led his people from Egyptian bondage. In his autobiography, *Towards the*

Mountain, and elsewhere, Paton draws his symbolic terminology for the Pilgrim Way from the Bible—from, as he says, "the vision of John of Patmos, of that world where there shall be no more death, neither sorrow, nor crying . . . "; or from the vision of Isaiah, ". . . where the wolf lies down with the lamb and they do not hurt or destroy in all that holy mountain" (12). Paton's autobiography, of which the title, *Towards the Mountain*, points toward the symbolic terminus, begins, nevertheless, with recollections of a childhood sense of harmony with nature.

The Hills of Home

There are writers with a strong sense of place who are moved more deeply than others by the natural life about them. Wordsworth, for example, felt nature as a numinous presence; and Robert Frost knew the familiar name of each bird, tree, and flower in the woods he loved to walk through. Paton, whose hobbies are gardening and bird-watching, has an equivalent knowledge of South African plants and birds and an active curiosity about the plants and birds of other countries. Yet, by a strange irony, the two persons whose intellects he most respected, and whose biographies he wrote, were both equally unmoved by natural beauty—a defect Paton was unwilling to overlook in them, or altogether forgive. Remarking on Archbishop Clayton's "imperviousness to scenery" he reveals one cause for puzzlement: "how he wedded land and history in his mind is beyond my powers to explain, because I need to see a country before I can understand what happened in it" (38). And Jan Hofmeyr, he found, valued, but did not appreciate, beauty: "he would eradicate slums, and build cities of noble buildings but with a moral and not an artistic purpose. . . . Were he a novelist, he would be unable to capture and set down the poignant beauty of human frailty."[6]

It is no accident, therefore, that Paton begins *Towards the Mountain* —before any mention of birth, parentage, or family circumstances— with a chapter on the place where he was born. In it he speaks of his intense childhood awakening to nature: "I cannot describe my early response to the beauty of hill and stream and tree as anything less than ecstasy." He recalls the child's delight in the brilliant flowers of Natal, "the scarlet fire-lilies" or "the magnificent orange clivia." But more than the sights—more even than the "once in a lifetime . . . glimpse of the small mpithi antelope, shy and delicate"—the sound of bird-calls delighted him. And it may be for the remembrance in them of the song of birds that he can say: "Robert Louis Stevenson expressed my deepest feelings in those lines from his poem 'To S. R. Crockett' ":

> Be it granted to me to behold you again in dying,
> Hills of Home! and to hear again the call;
> Hear about the graves of the martyrs the peewees crying,
> And hear no more at all.

He identifies the peewee, or peewit, as a member of the plover family. So is the titihoya whose plaintive anthem echoes through the opening chapter of *Cry, the Beloved Country*: "About you there is grass and bracken and you may hear the forlorn cry of the titihoya, one of the birds of the veld. . . . But the rich green hills break down. . . . The titihoya does not cry there any more."

He also recalls in the opening chapter of his autobiography the sound of the whippoorwill, known in Afrikaans as the *piet-my-vrou*. This is the bird heard in the lyrical passages of Chapter 7 of *Too Late the Phalarope* when Lieutenant Pieter van Vlaanderen, journeying back to the familiar countryside of his childhood, astonishes his young driver, Vorster, by his voluble excitement, saying "not once or twice but many times, this is the country, this is the country." The lieutenant advises the younger man to find a wife among those farms so that he might give up the police and ride round in the sun and the rain:

And what was better than that, for in the rain you could hear the plovers calling and the *piet-my-vrou* would cry from the kloof, which was like a hand suddenly plucking at the strings of the heart, so that your whole being shook and trembled; and why and why, why no one knew, it was the nature of man and of creation, that some sound long remembered from the days of innocence before the world's corruption, could open the door of the soul, flooding it with a sudden knowledge of the sadness and terror and beauty of man's home and the earth. (*TLP*, 47)

Paton says he concealed the intensity of his own early experience of nature from others: "In that sense I could have been described as a lonely child. But not as an unhappy one. I was too much in love with the world into which I had been born." He knew nothing in those carefree days of the worlds of race and politics: "Nor had I any idea that I lived in a country where no child of colour could aspire to the richness of the life I was going to lead" (6).

The World of Words

Paton, whose mother has already taught him how to read, went very early to what was then the equivalent of kindergarten. He passed rapidly through the elementary grades and entered high school three years younger than the average high-school freshman. His early childhood years were filled with books and reading to which he responded as intensely as he had responded to nature. He was impressed, first, by the Bible stories that were part of the life of his devoutly religious family, and then by such children's classics as *Tom Sawyer, Huckleberry Finn, Alice in Wonderland,* and *Through the Looking Glass,* Charles Kingsley's *Water Babies,* R. L. Stevenson's *Kidnapped* and *Treasure Island, Robinson Crusoe, The Swiss Family Robinson,* and works by Walter Scott, who was his father's favorite. His father, a court shorthand writer who aspired to be a poet, and who wrote verse for the local newspaper, also subscribed for him to two boys' weeklies from England: *Chums* and *Boys Own Paper*; and Paton says that as a child he did not want to leave the writing of stories to the authors he admired; he made his own little books from odd sheets of paper sewn together by his mother, and wrote stories in them. His interest in books remained alive in high school at an age when Tennyson's poems and Dickens's novels pleased him the most. The English Prize awarded him in his senior year was a sum of money with which he bought "eight handsomely bound novels of Dickens."

Looking back on his childhood in *Towards the Mountain* Paton says he had three things to be grateful for: "the opportunity to walk the hills of Pietermaritzburg, to know the stories and noble passages of the Bible, and to enter the world of words and books." His childhood was happy, he says, except for one thing: "the authoritarian and arbitrary rule of my father, which my mother tempered when she was able" (27).

Paton's Scottish-born father was a member of a fundamentalist sect, the Christadelphians, which his mother joined after her marriage to him. Members of the Christadelphian sect were law-abiding and uncompromisingly pacifist; but they forbade marriage with outsiders, regarded themselves as an elect, and looked forward to an earthly millenium when those worthy would enter the Kingdom. At home Paton's father was an authoritarian who lived by a narrow morality; insisted on obedience in trivial things; used physical punishment on his sons, and very likely, at times, on his wife. He was an embittered man who led a disappointed life and died tragically: his corpse half-submerged in a mountain stream, stripped of possessions and undiscovered for several weeks. Paton hated his father's violence and authoritarian constraint; and the memory of the father-son conflict colors some of the characterizations in his novels, particularly in *Too Late the Phalarope*. But his father, who had himself become a worker in Scotland at age fourteen, did nothing to thwart his son's desire for advanced education. He could not afford to send him to medical school—which was Paton's first wish—but he consented without protest to his accepting a government bursary available to undergraduates at the newly founded Natal University College who were prepared to train as teachers.

Natal University College: Front Row Center

As an undergraduate at Natal University College, Pietermaritzburg, Paton followed a science curriculum; but his required coursework in mathematics and physics did not occupy all of his energies. The college was both small and new, and Paton was prominent in almost every student activity. He joined the Students' Representative Council and became its president; and he may be seen in this office in a photograph in his autobiography captioned: "Students Representative Council, Natal University College, 1923. Author is front row centre." He had earlier joined the dramatic society; and he acted in, and also wrote, some of the plays produced by the society. *Towards the*

Mountain contains a photograph captioned: "Cast of 'His Excellency the Governor.' Natal University College, 1922. Author is front row centre"; but neither the caption not the text tells us that the author of the autobiography was also the author of this play in Shakespearean blank verse published in the *Natal University College Magazine*, October 1923, with the subtitle: "A circular drama in three short acts."[7] Paton regularly published verse—some signed, and some unsigned— in the college magazine. One of these early poems, "Old Til" (1923), and five poems that Paton contributed to the *Natal University College Magazine* during the next ten years are collected in *Knocking on the Door* (1975), and several others were published in the first edition of this study where the influence on them of poets then frequently anthologized was noted.[8] Paton confirms this view in *Towards the Mountain*, where he speaks of evenings spent with his friend Neville Nuttall reading Shakespeare, Milton, Wordsworth, Coleridge, Keats, Shelley, Byron, Tennyson, and Browning. Of Yeats, he says, they "knew nothing except possibly 'The Fiddler of Dooney' and 'The Lake Isle of Innisfree,' " and he adds: "but that is not strange because he did not get into the 1924 edition of *The Golden Treasury* or into *The Way of Poetry*, Drinkwater's anthology of the early 1920s" (63). T. S. Eliot did not get into those anthologies either; but Paton and his friends read the war poets: Wilfred Owen, Wilfred Gibson, Julian Grenfell, and Rupert Brooke. They thought Rupert Brooke "a greater poet than he was," says Paton, and they were "devoted to A. E. Housman, especially 'Loveliest of trees, the cherry now.' "

Some of the more successful of Paton's undergraduate poems— those that do not merely imitate admired models—reflect the influence of the war poets and of Housman; and they also introduce, for the first time, a real eye for local landscape. Paton and his undergraduate friends frequently took very long walks in the forty- to sixty-mile range over the Natal landscape; and on some of these walks they visited Boer War battlefields commemorated in Paton's early verse.

In two poems written in his eighteenth and nineteenth years, Paton steps out from the purely literary confines of the English anthology onto the landscape of Natal. The first, "Ladysmith (Midnight on the Battlefields)," is dated "Ladysmith, July 13th, 1921."[9] It is an elegiac lyric in the manner of Housman, addressed to a young soldier killed near the town of Ladysmith, where the Boer forces besieged the British during the Boer War. The emotion in the poem is directed not toward the cause of either warring party, but to the fallen young soldier who, significantly, is not identified as either Boer or British. The sixth and final quatrain—beginning like all the others with the refrain "Art lonely, son?"—runs as follows:

> Art lonely, son? the moon will pale,
> And o'er the hills come Dawn for thee,
> See, son, these wild veld-flowers I take
> And twine them on the cross of thee.

The second poem set in the Natal landscape is a ballad of a night train: "Song of the Northward-Bound."[10] This ballad of a lonely camper in the veld, composed in a pattern of ten well-paced, four-, five-, and six-line stanzas, is set in the vicinity of Colenso, scene of a battle where the Boer forces defeated the British in Natal under General Buller:

> Aye, oft in the hills of the thorn-tree belt
> I have heard the Northbound call.
> But where they sleep on the lonely veld
> It sounds the saddest of all.
>
> Dark, and a wind that rustles by me
> In the mist of a weary rain.
> Dark, and the dead that sleep by me
> In the sleep of Colenso plain.

Here again, as in "Ladysmith," the recollection of the Boer War raises no hint of provincial patriotism to Natal. Paton had been raised in a home that taught him to bear no enmity toward Afrikaners, and even the early poems reflect this. For the most part, however, although they have some qualities of technical excellence, the world these poems make manifest bears little resemblance to the world of Paton's later poems and fiction. The heritage they reflect is that of someone immersed in the English writers of the late nineteenth and early twentieth century, whose work was more or less contemporary at that time. For a Natal-born young man of British descent, they show exceptional restraint and tolerance when they advert to the Boer War; but, interestingly enough, they are silent on the theme of tribal African life, even though their author had frequently hiked and camped in the vicinity of Zululand and scattered African tribal reserves. In this regard, the lines already quoted from Arthur Jarvis's "Private Essay on the Evolution of a South African" in *Cry, the Beloved Country* are evocative: "One can ride, as I rode when I was a boy, over green hills and into great valleys. One can see, as I saw when I was a boy, the reserves of the Bantu people and see nothing of what was happening there at all. . . . It is only as one grows up that one learns there are other things here than sun and gold and oranges" (132).

Although Paton was not drawn to African or Indian life in Natal as a subject for his undergraduate poems, he records that it was during his years at the university that he began to understand and sympathize with African and Indian aspirations. In this respect he was influenced by a fellow student, Railton Dent, "the only human being for whom I ever felt some kind of worship" (*TM*, 58). Dent, the son of a Methodist missionary, had made up his mind early to devote his life to African education, and had served during the years of World War I as an uncertified principal of Edendale High School for African Boys. After the end of the war he entered the university to acquire further educational qualifications. Dent was six years older than Paton who looked up to him as a role model. It was Dent who invited Paton to join the Students' Christian Association at Natal University College and who taught him "that life must be used in the service of a cause greater than oneself"—a theme, Paton says, that runs through his autobiography, *Towards the Mountain*.

In 1924 the students of his university selected Paton to represent them at the first Imperial Student Conference, held in England at London and Cambridge. It was a highly formal affair with official government receptions of which Paton says in *Towards the Mountain*: "It was a new world to me. Lunches and dinners were given by the Government, the Lord Mayor, the Worshipful Company of Carpenters, teas . . . on the terrace of the House of Commons." On one occasion he says: "Six of us were received at the Palace of St. James by

Edward, Prince of Wales, later Edward the Eighth, later still the
Duke of Windsor" (*TM*, 79). The conference then adjourned from
London to Trinity College, Cambridge, for formal discussions. Two
of Paton's letters from this conference to the Student Representative
Council were published in the *Natal University College Magazine.*
The first of these speaks of the relations between the English-speaking
and Afrikaans-speaking groups in South Africa and is optimistic
about the role of student organizations in helping "to weld the whites
of South Africa into one race of South Africans."[11]

The second letter, a report from the conference's Commission on
Current Political Affairs, emphasizes the need for retaining the goodwill of India, which was likely to "secede from the Empire unless her
wrongs were redressed." This letter describes the students representing India at the conference as "fine, dignified, clever, and in
many cases handsome men"—a description calculated to impress his
fellow students in Natal in whose eyes all Indians were poorly educated laborers. If the Indian delegates impressed Paton, he apparently
impressed them, too, particularly by introducing a motion that
the Rhodes trustees no longer withhold Rhodes Scholarships from
Indians.

Essentially, what these letters reveal is that Paton as a young man
shared the views then common among South African liberals on the
relative urgency demanded by South Africa's several problems of
relations among races: first, reconciliation between the two white
"races," those who spoke English and those who spoke Afrikaans;
second, particularly in Natal, progress in the relations between
whites and Indians; and third, and much less urgent, relations
between whites and Africans. In Paton's own case, evolution to the
point where he urgently desired to turn this hierarchy on its head did
not take long.

Having fulfilled his duties as delegate to the Imperial Conference of
Students, Paton took advantage of his visit to Britain to visit the
habitats or the last resting places of some literary ghosts who haunt
his undergraduate poems. He concluded his final letter from the
conference with the reminder: "Poetic enthusiasts will writhe when I
say I spent some time at the ruins of Tintern Abbey, slept a night at
Ludlow, and am this afternoon going to Stratford." He toured Eng-

land and Scotland, chiefly by motorcycle, before returning to Natal to take up his first teaching assignment as a teacher of mathematics at Ixopo High School for White Students.[12]

Ixopo is a small rural community forty miles from Pietermaritzburg in the part of the Natal escarpment that Paton has described as it must have appeared to the first Voortrekkers: ". . . here was a paradisial country, a prodigal endowment of hills and valleys and rivers and streams, a rich lush grass abounding in flowers and game, a warm air full of coloured birds, a promise of reward and a foretaste of happiness to come."[13] Spurred by this locale and, he now thinks, by Hugh Walpole's Rogue Herries novels set in the English Lake District, he undertook two or three novels of white South African life set in the vicinity of Ixopo. He continued to write poetry, too, expressing a variety of moods. He contributed one substantial piece of light verse, "The New Physics,"[14] to a commemoration number of the *Natal University College Magazine.*

While teaching at Ixopo, Paton met his future wife, Doris Olive Francis. They were married at St. John's Anglican Church, Ixopo, on 2 July 1928. Paton was then a Methodist. At the time of the birth of their first son, David, he joined his wife's church, the Anglican Church of the Province of South Africa, which he adhered to devoutly and actively represented at national and international conferences from that time on. After his marriage Paton returned to Pietermaritzburg to teach at his old high school, Maritzburg College, where he remained until 1934. During these years, also, Paton helped to found the Students' Christian Association summer camps for boys; and he spent some time on Afrikaner farms in the Cape Province to improve his fluency in the Afrikaans language.

Winds of Change in South Africa

Shortly after Paton went to teach at Ixopo High School, his path crossed that of a man who was to have a profound effect on the course of his life both as a writer and as a man of affairs. This was Jan Hendrik Hofmeyr, who was Deputy Prime Minister of South Africa for some years prior to the Nationalist party election victory of 1948 that heralded the coming of *apartheid* as the official South African policy on race. During the fifteen years between 1949 and 1964, with unavoidable delays and interruptions, Paton worked on the great biography, *Hofmeyr* (published in the United States as *South African Tragedy: The Life and Times of Jan Hofmeyr*). Furthermore, from 1956 on, he undertook the burden of leading the South African Liberal party, founded in 1953, to keep Hofmeyr's liberal spirit alive in South African politics.

Jan Hofmeyr was a remarkable man. As a child he was an intellectual prodigy. Hofmeyr entered the university in Cape Town at the age of twelve and achieved a brilliant scholastic record there and subsequently at Oxford University. His later progress in public life was exceptional. At twenty-two he was a professor of classics; at twenty-four, president of a university, and at twenty-nine, Administrator of Transvaal Province—a position approximately equivalent to governor of a state in the United States. In 1933, at the age of thirty-four, he entered Parliament and was almost immediately appointed to the cabinet. At the outbreak of World War II he joined General Smuts in opposing Prime Minister Hertzog's bid to keep South Africa neutral; and, as wartime Minister of Finance and Acting Prime Minister, he became "the brain and power behind the South African war machine."

From his university days in Cape Town and Oxford on, Jan Hofmeyr had participated in the work of the Students' Christian Association, including the organization of clubs and camps for boys. Hofmeyr was an enthusiastic camper; throughout his life he preferred camping to any other form of vacation. In 1926, Paton, with two other high-school teachers, Reg Pearce and Cyril Armitage, established an annual boys' camp in Natal. This camp, the aim of which was "to win boys . . . to Christian principles in life and in society" (*H.*, 136; *S.A.T.*, 98), was an outgrowth of the earlier founding at Natal University College of a vigorous branch of the Students' Christian Association. Through common links with the parent association in Cape Town organized by his friend Oswin Bull, Hofmeyr came to Paton's second camp at Umgababa, "and then year after year to the new campsite on the Idomba River at Anerley, which site he helped the Association to buy and develop" (*H.*, 136; *S.A.T.*, 98).

In April 1934 Paton fell ill with enteric fever—a typhoid disease almost always fatal at that time. The only treatment was prolonged near-starvation. Paton spent eleven weeks in a hospital and a further twelve weeks in convalescence. Normally an active man, he had time during his six months of inactivity to think deeply. And there was much afoot in South Africa to think deeply about.

By 1934 the hopeful progress toward reconciliation between South Africans of British and Dutch origin, envisaged in Paton's letters from the Imperial Conference of Students ten years before, had not only halted; it had begun to go in reverse. The new prime minister, General Hertzog, had set afoot the parliamentary machinery that within two years was to remove African voters from the common roll in the Cape Province; and in his attitude toward the two white groups whom Louis Botha had tried to draw together he favored a "two-stream" policy that placed particular emphasis on separate schools and universities for those who spoke English and those who spoke Afrikaans. He thereby encouraged the perpetuation of separate national identities among whites of British and Dutch extraction. Beyond Hertzog was the splinter group of the Purified National party, led by Dr. D. F. Malan, who put the survival and ultimate triumph of the white Afrikaner "race" above any other consideration. In the late 1920s, legislation affecting Indians in South Africa had intensified, rather than alleviated, restrictions on this group. Some observers felt that the Hertzog election victory of 1929 had been won by an open and unashamed appeal to color prejudice. Furthermore, Hitler's racist theories emerging in Germany were being welcomed by those in South Africa sympathetic to the idea of a master race, and with the arrival in South Africa of increasing numbers of Jewish refugees from Europe there were unpleasant indications that anti-Semitism was on the rise.

Yet there were hopeful, even cheerful, signs for Paton to think about. In 1933 Jan Hofmeyr became a cabinet minister responsible for Education, as well as Interior and Public Health, in the new fusion government of Hertzog and Smuts. Hofmeyr, who on questions affecting Indian land tenure and Jewish immigration had stood firmly enough in Parliament to be identified by his opponents as the liberals' champion of Indians and Jews, now began a quiet revolution in the area of children's welfare. The improvements he introduced, since they were to apply impartially to institutions for children of all races and colors, were revolutionary in South Africa. Chief among these improvements was a basic shift in emphasis in the treatment of child offenders, so that reformatory institutions were no longer to be regarded as places of punishment, but of education. Hofmeyr took the first step in this direction in 1934, when he transferred responsibility for all reformatory institutions from the Department of Prisons to the Department of Education and prepared to appoint new personnel to supervise the transformation of the three reformatories—for white, for colored (mixed blood), and for black African offenders—into educational institutions.

While convalescing from enteric fever Paton submitted applications for all three of the new positions created for reformatory principals. When he received his appointment in 1935, it was to the post at Diepkloof Reformatory in faraway Johannesburg—a crowded, prisonlike institution for about seven hundred delinquent African youths ranging in age from ten to twenty-one. So the "novels of country life" that occupied him at Ixopo and Pietermaritzburg were laid aside. So was work on his thesis for a master's degree in education for which he had already completed the comprehensive examinations—rated *summa cum laude* by his examiner. They would not be taken up again. But the books he studied for the M.Ed., including McDougall's *Abnormal Psychology*, John Dewey's *Democracy and Education*, and works by Freud, A. S. Neill, and Montessori, no doubt contributed to the insight into complex character motivation Paton revealed in his novels—particularly so contradictory an inner personality as that of Pieter van Vlaanderen in *Too Late the Phalarope*. One book he read for this course of study, Paton says, changed the direction of his life. This was Cyril Burt's *The Young Delinquent*.

Chapter Two
With Freedom
as an Instrument

Diepkloof Reformatory

Diepkloof Reformatory, Johannesbrug, had long been a prison farm; and when Paton took over his duties there in July 1935 its detention buildings were old and dilapidated. (Mahatma Gandhi had been imprisoned there in 1913 for leading a march of 2,700 Indians from Natal into the Transvaal in nonviolent protest against laws forbidding Indians to cross provincial boundaries.) Diepkloof occupied a thousand acres of farmland on the outskirts of Johannesburg between the white suburb of Willowdene and such African slum townships as Newclare, the place described in *Cry, the Beloved Country* as Claremont, "the garbage heap of the proud city." Claremont was the place where Stephen Kumalo found his sister Gertrude reduced to prostitution and the brewing and selling of illegal liquor. As Kumalo's guide, the Reverend Theophilus Msimangu, described it, Claremont was a place where in the aftermath of a police raid, "you can see the liquor running in the streets. You can smell it, you can smell nothing else in that place" (23).

Diepkloff was still run by the Department of Prisons when Paton was first appointed to supervise its transformation into a school. It was staffed by sixty armed wardens; and, indeed, Paton's office was chief warden until the institution's transference to the Department of Education was completed. He was then named principal. Diepkloof's inmates—four hundred African youths aged from seven to twenty-one, who had been convicted of offenses ranging from petty theft to rape and murder—were housed in wood-and-iron buildings surrounded on all sides by a high barbed-wire fence. At night they were locked in, twenty to a room, "with one bucket full of water, and another bucket for urination and defecation." In the mornings "the stench . . . was unspeakable." Paton first persuaded the fearful prison staff to leave the dormitories unlocked at night. This permitted the lavatories to be used when needed, and as a result "typhoid fever, which had been the scourge of the reformatory and the cause of many deaths, almost completely disappeared" (*FYD*, 110).

Apart from his own qualities of mind and spirit, there was little in Paton's background to prepare him for this new experience. The boys he had taught during his years in Ixopo and Pietermaritzburg—in an environment of great natural beauty—were the children of comparatively well-to-do white families. Those now coming under his care were chiefly products of African slums, habituated to poverty and convicted of serious crimes. Yet he saw the prospect before him as a creative task: "Then in 1935 I went to Diepkloof Reformatory, and that was the end of writing, because the transformation of a virtual prison into a school required all one's creative energy."[1]

Paton's appointment to Diepkloof also caused some domestic upheaval and a strain on his marriage. Dismayed at the assignment, his wife, Dorrie, at first refused to be uprooted from her beloved Natal, or to face the unfamiliar world of urban, black Johannesburg. It was a month before she followed him there with their infant son, David. But they were reconciled and came to regard Diepkloof as "home"; and as their family life grew stronger, so did their commitment to a nonracial ideal. "It was at Diepkloof," said Paton, "that we began to feel that the color-bar that ruled South African life was unendurable. So far as we were able we threw it out of our lives" (*FYD*, 130).

When he undertook, and indeed succeeded in, the challenging task of transforming a prison into a remedial community, Paton probably did not anticipate a day when Diepkloof Reformatory would survive only through the medium of his own writings on penal reform (some of them collected in *Knocking on the Door*, 1975) and his later fiction and drama. Portions of *Cry, the Beloved Country*, the play *Sponono*, and several of his short stories discussed in Chapter 5 are based on particulars of Diepkloof. But Diepkloof itself no longer exists. It became what it was, a unique experiment in education, through Jan Hofmeyr's action transferring reformatories for youths of all races from the Department of Prisons to the Department of Education. It ceased to exist in 1958, when the government of the day—carrying out the policies of Dr. Verwoerd—closed it down and transferred its 800 African inmates to rural Youth Labour Camps where they would be employed in farm labor under the supervision of warders.

Paton had conceived of Diepkloof as a place of education and rehabilitation based on "increasing freedom, increasing responsibility, increasing privilege, and increasing temptation," because he felt there could be no proof of the sincerity of the offender's intention to reform until he could at least resist the temptation to run away when free to do so. This freedom was arrived at by stages. Newly committed boys were housed in a general "closed" dormitory. When they proved themselves trustworthy, they were transferred to cottages, in groups of six to eight, under the care of a house-father and house-mother. They received immediate recognition for good behavior, and "free" boys wore distinguishing badges on their pockets, as in the play *Sponono*. As a further step in preparing them for reentry into society, these free boys could, in time, have weekend leave to go home to their families or friends in the Johannesburg area. The most trustworthy senior boys were permitted to live and work outside Diepkloof in placement hostels in Orlando and Jabavu townships where they paid a small part of their earnings for their keep. Of the ten thousand boys given home leave during Paton's years at Diepkloof, only 1 percent did not return. One of these killed a white woman who surprised him in the pantry of her home—as Absolom Kumalo was surprised by Arthur Jarvis in *Cry, the Beloved Country*.

Since the ages of boys committed to Diepkloof ranged from ten to twenty-one, there were different arrangements for the younger and older groups. The younger boys spent their days chiefly in formal schooling. Paton had special affection for these younger ones, and his compassion for them is manifested in his story "Ha'penny" and also his poem "To a small boy who died at Diepkloof Reformatory."[2] Paton repeatedly recommended a separate institution for these smaller boys, for their own benefit, and also to relieve the crowded conditions at Diepkloof. Shortly before he resigned his principalship in 1948, the Department of Education accepted his recommendations to establish a separate school for these younger boys. The money was, in fact, voted for this new school, which was to be called the Alan Paton School. But within a month of this decision, there was a change in government in South Africa. Dr. Malan became prime minister, and the reformatory for African boys was transferred from the Department of Education to the Department of Native Affairs. The new administration disapproved of the project for the Alan Paton School and it was abandoned.

Within three years of his appointment at Diepkloof, Paton was able to report: "We have removed all the more obvious aids to detention. The dormitories are open all night; the great barred gate is gone."[3] The necessary support for his experiments came first from the senior officials in the Department of State responsible for reformatory institutions before 1948; and he has recorded that he had the privilege of working for thirteen years under a department "that had tried ably and honestly to give full effect to the provisions of the magnificent Children's Act of 1937." Paton felt that this act, piloted through Parliament by Jan Hofmeyr, changed reformatory institutions out of all recognition through its basic premise that child offenders were in need of care, not of punishment. In his *Hofmeyr* he describes this act as "one of the most enlightened measures of its kind in the world." Added to the valuable advantages of this act was the unusual freedom permitted him in the practical application of its provisions. He has said on this point: "I even had the extraordinary experience, almost unknown to Public Servants, of administering Diepkloof Reformatory for some years under no regulations at all, and this meant a freedom to experiment that comes to few of us in our lifetime."[4]

He also received another kind of support, invaluable to him in developing his system of restoring offenders to useful and dignified roles in society. This support came from such groups as the South African Institute of Race Relations and its affiliated organization, the Penal Reform League. These groups provided him with platforms for lectures in their symposiums and the opportunity for writing in the pages of their journals. The also brought out his two penal reform pamphlets, *The Non-European Offender* (1945) and *Freedom as a Reformatory Instrument* (1948), which have been reprinted in *Knocking on the Door* (1975). His pioneering work received similar recognition from the South African liberal fortnightly *Forum*, whose editors commissioned him to prepare a series of articles during 1943 and 1944 on punishment and crime, and the prospects for postwar reform in South Africa. It should be remembered that this encouraging climate still prevailed—with what appeared to be excellent prospects for the future—when Paton wrote *Cry, the Beloved Country* in 1946.

The chief opposition to Paton's experiments came from the self-righteous observers who believed that crime could be ruthlessly "stamped out." Representatives of this view found Paton's ideas impractical, and his attitude to young offenders sentimental. They preferred their own "realistic" view: that the function of a reformatory—particularly one for delinquent African youths—was to convey, unequivocally, through strictness and deprivation, what Paton calls "the great lesson that crime does not pay." He has noted in his *Hofmeyr* that "one of the sourest observers" of the Diepkloof experiment was Dr. Hendirk Verwoerd, the architect of *apartheid*, then editor of the newspaper *Die Transvaler*, who described Diepkloof "as a place for pampering rather than education, as the place indeed where one said *'please'* and *'thank you'* to the black *misters*."[5] It was Dr. Verwoerd, then Minister for Native Affairs, who closed down Diepkloof and replaced it by a system of rural labor camps in 1958—the same year that he became Prime Minister of South Africa.

The Qualities of the Hero in Literature

When Paton was attacked for relying on freedom rather than punishment at Diepkloof, he defended his approach by saying: ". . . much more dangerous is our present unscientific belief that punishment can deter men from evil and incline them to good."[6] This awareness of an equal human capacity for evil, as well as for good, is one of the chief characteristics of his literary work. There are no flatly "heroic" or wholly admirable characters in his fiction. Even Stephen Kumalo in *Cry, the Beloved Country*, whom some commentators have described as "saintly," has his petty weaknesses: a touch of vanity, and a tendency to seek to hurt those who have hurt him. And Pieter van Vlaanderen in *Too Late the Phalarope* has an elusive and enigmatic duality of character compounded of both great strength and great weaknesses.

The notion of "the hero" in literature implies "the kind of human being who most deserves to be celebrated, remembered, and, if possible, imitated."[7] If no character in Paton's fiction represents the sum of desirable human qualities, his novels nevertheless presuppose certain ideal qualities of behavior and outlook necessary for any progress toward an ideal South African society. The characters in Paton's novels may grope their way toward this ideal or they may attain or reject these qualities to greater or less degree. But only one character comes close to epitomizing them and he is already dead when we encounter him. This is Arthur Jarvis, the murdered man in *Cry, the Beloved Country*. What we learn of him from others, the writing he has left behind, and the account of his funeral that draws mourners of many races, creeds, and social organizations—all these qualities (epitomized as we shall shortly see in Mrs. Edith Rheinallt Jones) represent, in summary form, "the highest and best kind of things to strive for in a country like South Africa." In short, the ideal person in Paton's novels incorporates qualities of heart and mind that found practical expression in South Africa in such pursuits as the work of the Institute of Race Relations, or in the devotion to the spirit of liberty represented by the journal *Forum* which supported Jan Hofmeyr's liberal views.

Paton's series of six articles on crime and punishment published in *Forum* during 1943—44 proposed that the best way to deter crime is to restore to each person a feeling of social significance: "To mean something in the world is the deepest hunger of the human soul, deeper than any bodily hunger or thirst, and when a man has lost it he is no longer a man. . . ."[8] Another great way to combat crime, according to this series, is to reform society itself, so that every man can take his place in it with dignity:

There is one supreme reason why men do not commit crime and that is because they have goals, interests, ideals, homes, children, savings schemes. The home, the church, the association, have given them worthy aims and have expressed—and continue to express—social approval of their lives and actions. They do not commit crime—not because they are afraid—but because they are socially significant.[9]

If we turn from this remark to the account of Arthur Jarvis's funeral in *Cry, the Beloved Country*, and note the number of representatives, and the messages of condolence, from the many groups and associations he participated in actively in both the white and black communities, we may observe how the "good" man in Paton's novels is one who works in practical ways to contribute fullness, meaning, and greater social significance to the lives of others.

There is, of course, no single prototype among Paton's acquaintances for the ideal character in his fiction. Hofmeyr, for all his brilliant clarity of intellect, had little aptitude for social fellowship, or for establishing personal contacts across the boundaries of race. Yet his example of moral courage—his unflinching championship of the principles of justice—furnishes an essential quality of the ideal character. So also does Alfred Hoernlé, who is mentioned by name in *Cry, the Beloved Country* and described in Paton's "Author's Note" as "a great and courageous fighter for justice."

Jan Hofmeyr, Professor Hoernlé, and others may well supply some of the qualities of the ideal character in Paton's early fiction, but in the particular instance of the characterization of Arthur Jarvis in *Cry, the Beloved Country* he appears to have had in mind certain memories of Mrs. Edith Rheinallt Jones. In addition to her work for the Institute of Race Relations, which she and her husband helped to found, Mrs. Jones was active in such pursuits as directing a hostel for African young women, and in organizing troops of Wayfarers—the equivalent of Girl Scouts—for African schoolgirls. She continued these activities even after doctors had warned her that the state of her health required that she forgo all activity. During World War II Paton agreed to drive her on her inspections of outlying troops of Wayfarers in Transvaal tribal villages. On one such occasion, probably the last, they had to make their final approach to an isolated village on foot—an exertion that caused Mrs. Jones painful distress. But it was not so much her uncomplaining courage that impressed Paton as the realization that the personal friendship between Mrs. Jones and Mrs. Takalani, the African teacher in charge of the village troop, needed none of the conventional surface politeness so characteristic of social contacts across the boundaries of race in a race-conscious country. He says: "At that time my own relations with black people were extremely polite, but I realized that these two had long passed that stage." Theirs was not a friendship between women of different races but simply a nonracial friendship.

A month later Mrs. Jones died. Her funeral made a very deep impression on Paton, for he felt it provided a momentary glimpse of racial unity in South Africa. He has referred to the emotion he experienced at this funeral on more than one occasion in his writings: in his 1951 Peter Ainslee Memorial Lecture, *Christian Unity*, for instance; and, in greater detail, as the deepest experience of his life, in "A Deep Experience" (1961), which is reprinted in *The Long View*. It seems reasonable to suggest that the account of the funeral of Arthur Jarvis in *Cry, the Beloved Country*, and of its profound effect on his father, James Jarvis, draws on this deep experience. Paton recalls that St. George's Presbyterian Church, Johannesburg, was crowded for the funeral services of Mrs. Jones: "Black man, white man, coloured man, European and African and Asian, Jew and Christian and Hindu and Moslem, all had come there to honor her memory—their hates and their fears, their prides and their prejudices, all for this moment forgotten." Looking back, twenty years later when, under *apartheid*, socially mixed gatherings of any kind were either illegal or impossible, at "all South Africa reconciled under the roof of this Church," Paton recalls:

> As for me, I was overwhelmed. I had seen a vision, which was never to leave me, illuminating the darkness of the days through which we live now. . . . What life had failed to give so many of these people, this woman had given them, an assurance that their work was known and of good report, and that they were not nameless or meaningless. And man has no hunger like this one. Had they all come, no church would have held them all; the vast, voiceless multitude of Africa, nameless and obscure, moving with painful ascent to that self-fulfilment no human being may with justice be denied. . . .
>
> In that church one was able to see, beyond any possibility of doubt, that what this woman had striven for was the highest and best kind of thing to strive for in a country like South Africa. [10]

This deep experience occurred in 1944, toward the close of World War II. It bore fruit for Paton as a writer two years later when Edith

Rheinallt Jones's lifelong devotion to restoring in others their sense of self-respect and human dignity suggested aspects of the character of Arthur Jarvis in *Cry, the Beloved Country*. But it also deepened his own understanding of the attitude toward his fellow men that he describes as a "non-racial" attitude. He says of the effect of this experience: "I knew that I would never again be able to think in terms of race and nationality. I was no longer a white person but a member of the human race"; and he sums up the effect of this deep experience on the evolution of his own racial attitudes with the remark: "I had never been militantly white, but now I became militantly non-racial."

Paton had volunteered for military service at the outbreak of World War II, but his offer was turned down on the grounds that his occupation was essential. He nevertheless added numerous voluntary duties to the exacting demands of his work at Diepkloof. Besides his activities for the Institute of Race Relations and such practical endeavors as his assistance to Edith Rheinallt Jones, he joined in the work of the combined YMCA and Talbot House (Toc-H) War Services and became National Chairman of this voluntary organization which provided somewhat similar services for South African combat forces as the combination of the Post Exchange and the Red Cross volunteer workers did for American servicemen. Even though Paton was not directly involved in military action, the war brought him personal tragedy. His only brother, Athol, was killed in the battle of El Wak on the Kenya-Somaliland border, 16 December 1940, at the beginning of the campaigns against Italian forces in Somaliland and Abyssinia.

Perspective from Trondheim

Shortly after the war ended, Paton felt that his future lay with penal reform. With his friend Jan Hofmeyr still deputy prime minister and likely to be prime minister, he had a realistic hope of being appointed Director of Prisons. He therefore decided to take a leave of absence from Diepkloof Reformatory to undertake a study of penal and correctional practice in Europe and America at his own expense. He set out, therefore, in the latter half of 1946 on an eight-month tour of penal institutions in Britain, Sweden, Canada, and the United States.

Before beginning his tour of penal systems, Paton, on his arrival in England, first attended an international conference of the Society of Christians and Jews. The conference opened in London with an address by Reinhold Niebuhr—"the most enthralling speaker" Paton ever heard—and it continued at Oxford, where he met "the man become saint": Rabbi Leo Baeck, who had survived the concentration camps.[11] He then set out on his tour in the course of which he frequently found himself alone on long journeys or in hotel rooms, particularly in the Scandinavian countries where he did not know the language. His autobiography, *Towards the Mountain* (1980), reports in detail how, in these circumstances, the urge to write creative fiction returned. So at Trondheim in Norway he began to write *Cry, the Beloved Country*. He continued working on it in Sweden, Canada, and the United States, for the most part in hotel rooms. He finished it some three months later in San Francisco. In that city, on 23 December 1946, Paton met Aubrey Burns and his wife, Marigold, of Fairfax, California, during a social gathering at the offices of the National Conference of Christians and Jews.

On 25 December, the Burnses invited Paton to spend Christmas with them in Marin County. He accepted the offer on condition they agreed to read a novel he was working on. The Burnses read Paton's handwritten manuscript, helped choose its title by lot, and arranged to have it typed and submitted to publishers before he departed from Halifax, Nova Scotia, on a freighter early in February. Aubrey Burns sent some chapters of the typescript to Maxwell Perkins, the famous editor at Charles Scribner's Sons who had worked with Ernest Hemingway and F. Scott Fitzgerald. Perkins accepted the book. For their part in bringing the novel into print, Paton arranged that the Burnses should receive a share of the royalties as an agents' fee, and he dedicated the American edition of the book as follows: "To Aubrey and Marigold Burns of Fairfax, California." The British and South African editions of the work were dedicated: "To my Wife and to my friend of many years Jan Hendrick Hofmeyr."

Chapter Three

Of Faith and Fear:
Cry, the Beloved Country

The Plain and Simple Truth

Africa has seen extraordinary political change since *Cry, the Beloved Country* was written in 1946. In that year, only three territories in the entire continent had fully independent governments: Egypt, Liberia, and the Union of South Africa. Three other territories, including Ethiopia, had been wrested from Italian rule during World War II; but most of the continent was still ruled directly by the major European colonial powers: France, Britain, Portugal, Belgium, and Spain. Within twenty years, however, more than forty African nations had achieved independence from colonial rule. In some instances turmoil accompanied change. This was so, for example, in the former Belgian Congo at the time of independence in 1960; and later, in Uganda under Idi Amin. But, for the most part, the new nations adopted democratic constitutions; African diplomatic missions sat at the United Nations; and African heads of state participated in international meetings. The freedoms and prerogatives accompanying self-rule did not extend to Africans living in white-ruled South Africa who, together with the Indian and Cape Coloured populations, were subject, under *apartheid*, to increasing control and restriction.

In the 1980s a new generation has grown up in Africa, and this generation faces challenges and tensions that differ greatly from those of the immediately postwar colonial period (including the problem of the continued presence of *apartheid* on the continent). Therefore no novel written in the 1940s is likely to reflect with any exactness conditions now prevailing in Africa; and Paton's *Cry, the Beloved Country* is no exception. But it is still true to say that this novel portrays with remarkable authenticity a segment of South African life during a brief period following the end of World War II. The work succeeds—and it still appeals to a very wide readership—because Paton effectively endowed his regional portrait with a measure of universal human significance. The realities of the postwar South African setting in which the events of the novel take place were in all likelihood unfamiliar to most readers; but the theme of social disintegration, and the countertheme of the need to restore, could evoke sympathetic understanding in a world exhausted by war. These themes are worked out in the novel through two complementary actions: Stephen Kumalo's physical search for his son, Absalom, and James Jarvis's intellectual search for the spirit of his son, Arthur. In each case, the journey, once undertaken, leads to an inner, spiritual awakening.

The story that sustains these deeper themes and contrasts is a very simple one. Stephen Kumalo, aging Zulu pastor of a small Anglican mission church in the tribal village of Ndotsheni, sets out for the unfamiliar world of industrial Johannesburg to seek his sister Gertrude, who had gone there, years before, to look for her husband and had not been heard from again. He hopes also to discover his son, Absalom, who went to look for Gertrude and failed to return. And he has the further hope of finding his brother, John, who, like so many others from the village, had gone to Johannesburg and had not returned. He finds all three. But each is enmeshed in a web of moral degeneration, and his hopes of reuniting them in the old close-knit tribal family are defeated.

He finds his son, Absalom, a confessed murderer. The victim is Arthur Jarvis, a young white man noted in Johannesburg for his devotion to the cause of racial justice, and the only son of James Jarvis, the white farmer whose land occupies the fertile high ground above the barren, eroded valley of Ndotsheni. Between the discovery of the murder and the completion of the trial, the paths of the bereft fathers cross. Each seeks to understand his son's divergence from accustomed ways—the one fallen from the standards of the church his father served, the other committed to a vision of racial justice quite alien to his father's conventional assumptions. The elders return home, the wiser, if sadder, like T. S. Eliot's Magus, "no longer at ease in the old dispensation." Their mutual recognition of each other's suffering engenders a hitherto unthought-of sense of shared humanity. So simple a narrative framework can achieve literary significance only to the degree that a writer finds a fitting artistic vehicle for the depth of his vision and the power of his initial emotional mood.

Novelists, while engaged in composition, struggle to reconcile a desire to represent some human situation truthfully, with a desire to arrange their materials in the best, and most interesting, order. For some writers, the technical matters of style and arrangement are a primary concern. Others, impelled by the urgency of their concern with the human situation, adopt fictional or dramatic forms to express heartfelt convictions. While it is also a successful artistic achievement, *Cry, the Beloved Country* is a product of this second urge, which Paton once described as a desire to write "books that would stab South Africa in the conscience." He draws attention to the moral aspect of his purpose in his "Author's Note" on fictional persons and events, when he states: "In these respects therefore the story is not true, but considered as a social record it is the plain and simple truth" (vii).

In the light of the broad facts of the South African social record in 1945—46, the period of the novel's setting, this claim is certainly justified. Even those who did not share Paton's views on race relations would admit that the conditions encountered by the aged Zulu priest, while searching for his son, really existed. It was true that the land in tribal reserves, like the countryside around his tribal village, Ndotsheni, was poor, badly eroded, and incapable of sustaining its people; that the tribal reserves were inhabited chiefly by old men and women because the young men were away working in the mines and the industries of Johannesburg; and that overcrowded urban slums and lack of opportunity for employment contributed to growing frustration and crime.

There seems little doubt, therefore, that Paton turned to literary creation in a Trondheim hotel, in part out of nostalgia for his homeland and, in part, impelled by the urgency of what he had to say about social and moral disintegration in South African black society. An article of his that appeared in *Forum*, 15 December 1945, almost on the eve of his departure for the tour of Europe and the United States during which he wrote *Cry, the Beloved Country*, is of particular interest in this regard, for it shows that the basic theme of the novel was uppermost in his mind. This brief article, "Who Is Really to Blame for the Crime Wave in South Africa?",[1] is remarkable for two reasons: first, for the urgency of its tone; and second, because it contains the essential themes of *Cry, the Beloved Country*, prior to their embodiment in fictional form.

Paton began his article on crime by warning against the tendency to dismiss outbreaks of crime among Africans as part of a general postwar phenomenon, thereby ignoring the more important underlying cause, the disintegration of tribal society under the impact of Western economy and culture. "For a long time," he says, "the full dangers were not seen, but fathers and sons and daughters went to work and sometimes never came back. . . ." In the course of time, Africans attempted to set up new homes in cities, but, robbed of the powerful support of tribal custom, these families "began to experience with bewilderment and shame the shocks of disobedient children, pregnant daughters, delinquent sons." The atmosphere of overcrowded slums accelerated this decay of home life which, he says, also decayed in the tribal reserves, "where men did not come back, and where women went away to look for them and often found someone else." This is, essentially, the picture of disintegration incorporated into Book One of *Cry, the Beloved Country*.

The second part of the article turns to the question, "How is society to be restored?" And it responds: "Moral and spiritual decay can be stopped only by moral and spiritual means." Restoration requires education, and opportunities for work, and the growth of self-respect so as to create a climate where decency and morality can flourish. He repeats the insistent theme of his earlier *Forum* articles: "Men obey the laws when they are pursuing worthy goals, working for some good purpose, making the most of their seventy years, using their gifts."

Besides focusing on the general climate of disintegration, *Cry, the Beloved Country* draws on other realities of the South African social condition of 1945−46. This is typical of Paton's fictional method, which, characteristically—as in *Too Late the Phalarope* (1953) and *Ah, But Your Land Is Beautiful* (1981)—seeks materials in the actualities of South African life. In *Cry, the Beloved Country* these include the building of Shanty Town, the bus boycott, the discovery of rich new gold deposits at Odendaalsrust, and the air of frenzied excitement that the discovery engendered on the stock market and in Johannesburg as a whole. The actual record also included such less publicized endeavors as the work of the Anglican clergy, both black and white, at the Mission House, Sophiatown; and of the welfare workers at Diepkloof Reformatory and at "the wonderful place," Enzenzeleni, where the blind were rehabilitated.

In building the fictional world of his characters Paton also drew on his memories of certain actual persons. He reveals in *Towards the Mountain* that his recollections of a humble old clergyman who used to visit his son at Diepkloof Reformatory contributed to the characterization of Stephen Kumalo: "The old man wore his minister's suit when he paid his visits and made no attempt to hide the fact that a priest of the church had fathered a delinquent son" (271). The ambivalent character of Kumalo's daughter, Gertrude—torn between the call of the streets and the pious aspiration to become a nun—owed much to Jacky, a boy at Diepkloof who claimed that a voice called him to be a priest, but absconded on the eve of the day on which he was to start a new life as Gertrude does in the novel. And Professor Horton Davies has pointed out that Father Trevor Huddleston of the Rosettenville Mission House of the Anglican Community of the Resurrection provided the model for the sympathetic portrait of Father Vincent, and also that some of Paton's own qualities are embodied in the murdered man, Arthur Jarvis: "The wide interests of the man and the very titles of his cherished library and the significant portraits on the wall of his study, these are as autobiographical as the social Credo and the ethical platform of Alan Paton."[2]

Undoubtedly Arthur Jarvis's library, with its books on birds and flowers as well as on race relations and literature, is modeled on the author's own collection, for Paton's hobbies included bird-watching and gardening. The wide interests of Jarvis also parallel those of the author, who was associated with such organizations as Toc-H, YMCA, the Transvaal Non-European Boys' Clubs, and the Society of Christians and Jews. Yet the character of Arthur Jarvis in *Cry, the Beloved Country* is not simply a self-portrait. Jarvis is a representative type, incorporating the admirable traits of a number of people whom Paton admired. Nevertheless, Paton's identification of his models in

Towards the Mountain substantiates the view that he drew on incidents and persons from actual life for fictional material—a method that adds to the air of authenticity in the novel's social settings.

Cry, the Beloved Country also probes the no less real problem of the subconscious springs of racial attitudes that, tinged with "the bondage of fear," inhibit justice and the inclination to restore. It reveals one fear in particular, diagnosed by the thoughtful young Zulu priest, Msimangu, who had no hate for any man. Speaking of the whites he says: "I have one great fear in my heart, that one day when they turn to loving, they will find we are turned to hating" (40). The intensity and pervasiveness of this fear is one of the central themes of the novel. Fear shows in the eyes of the God-fearing as well as of evil-doers. There is fear, too, in the daily newspapers. The land itself is enveloped in fear. And fingers of fear reach toward the future: "Cry, the beloved country, for the unborn child that is the inheritor of our fear. Let him not love the earth too deeply" (80). Commenting on this passage more than thirty years later in *Towards the Mountain*, Paton said that if the child loves the earth too deeply he cannot ask immunity from pain: "This is what the visitors from America and Britain and Germany and other countries mean when they say to me, 'Ah, but your country is beautiful.' They mean, 'But why is it so full of pain?' " And he adds: "I am sometimes astonished when I remember that these words were written in 1946, and that it took many of the white people of South Africa thirty years to acknowledge their truth, when black school children started rioting in the great black city of Soweto on June 16, 1976, on the day after which, of all the hundred thousand days of our written history, nothing would be the same again" (293). In his first novel, where these events of 1976 were unforeseen, the intense concern with a climate of fear nevertheless heightens the dramatic conflict of love and hate; for many of the characters know, or come to know, that fear engenders hatred, and that only through love can fear be cast out.

The Artistic Problem

It would be difficult to imagine a landscape or a point on the earth's surface so different in every way from South Africa as Trondheim, Norway. Yet it may have been fortunate for the artist in Alan Paton that Trondheim was the place where he undertook to compose *Cry, the Beloved Country*. This was not because of any direct influence other than that of loneliness and longing for home. True, he had read John Steinbeck's *The Grapes of Wrath* in Stockholm, and his sidetrip to Norway was prompted by a wish to visit the countryside depicted in Knut Hamsun's grimly realistic novel *Growth of the Soil*; but he says he did not consciously adapt anything from either work except Steinbeck's "style of rendering conversations, indicating by a preliminary dash that a speech was about to begin, and omitting all inverted commas" (*TM*, 269). What may have mattered more was that distance permitted a perspective that allowed him to see his own country and the struggles of its diverse peoples as a whole. It is essentially this overall point of view that makes *Cry, the Beloved Country* a unique artistic object: a dramatic manifestation of the agony of a country in which the spirit of South Africa hovers always on stage and dominates the human actors like the ever-present, threatening and life-giving force of the sea in J. M. Synge's play *Riders to the Sea*.

Many readers of *Cry, the Beloved Country* are struck by the simplicity of its language and the rhythmic quality of its prose style. Some of its rhythms—dependent on parallel phrases and repetitions—evoke translations of the Psalms. Because of this, the style of *Cry, the Beloved Country* has frequently been described as "biblical." This description is only partly accurate because it implies that Paton's is a naturally rhythmic style, and that the whole novel is written in one style.

But the novel has a wide variety of styles. The element that may strike readers first as having a flavor of originality is the evocation of the rhythms of Zulu speech that appears, chiefly, in Stephen Kumalo's speech and thought, and in dialogue among African characters. For an obvious contrast, however, one should look at the style of the elder Harrison in Book Two. Harrison is almost a caricature of the typical colonialist-minded United Party man from Johannesburg's English-speaking commercial community, hidebound by prejudice. He parrots hackneyed ideas about "the native problem." He speaks almost wholly in clichés, and is quite incapable of examining them from a fresh viewpoint. He is like the "stone age" neighbor in Robert Frost's "Mending Wall," who cannot go behind his father's saying: "Good fences make good neighbors."

For a stylistic counterpoint to Harrison's conventional common-places, one should turn to the documents left behind by the murdered man, Arthur Jarvis. Anyone familiar with the writings of Alfred Hoernlé—whose spirit frequently walks abroad in the novel—would probably recognize in their trenchant arguments, not only echoes of the ideas, but of the personal "synoptic" style that Hoernlé sought to develop.[3] One could pursue these instances of characterization through style further: to the speech of James Jarvis, for instance, or of the village schoolmaster in Ndotsheni, and find that Paton's ear seems extraordinarily well tuned to the varied rhythms of speech, and also that he employs differences in speech patterns to give individuality to his characters, and to the cacophonous voices that clamor in his choruses.

Even though *Cry, the Beloved Country* is not written in one style and rhythm but in many styles and rhythms, there is, none-theless, a dominant style associated with the book. This is the pattern of speech with a marked poetic quality accorded to Kumalo and the African characters generally, and also to some extent employed in the lyric passages voiced from outside the action. This quality, depending to a degree on the sound and syntax of spoken Zulu, can be viewed as a poetic invention designed to carry over into English the effects of the sound and idiom of African speech.

What Paton achieves has a close analogy in the poetic language of J. M. Synge's Irish plays. In the work of both writers the "dialect" is a poetic invention. J. M. Synge described the language of the naturalistic drama and fiction of his day as "dealing with the realities of life in joyless and pallid words," and proposed the use of the more vivid speech of rural Ireland. Paton employs an African equivalent, and both Synge and Paton affirm the value of poetic qualities in literature in strikingly similar ways. Synge declared: "In a good play every speech should be as fully flavoured as a nut or an apple, and such speeches cannot be written by anyone who works among people who have shut their lips on poetry." And Paton, reflecting perhaps on the theme of his novel, has said: "If you write in terms of poetry, fears and inhibitions disappear."[4]

The Voices of South Africa

It is not surprising that Paton wrote *Cry, the Beloved Country* quickly, since he already had all the material in mind. What is surprising, however, is that he wrote it so well. The stroke of genius was his hitting upon a lyric and dramatic framework—none of it thought out in advance—that could incorporate more than the realistic "slice of life" ordinarily offered by novels of social purpose like those of Steinbeck or Hamsun. From the perspective of Trondheim the whole of South Africa lay before the artist's inner eye like a map. He could envision the landscape of Natal beloved from childhood, and the contrasting bustle of Johannesburg, the City of Gold, a magnet for Africans from tribal areas seeking a new way of life. Even more significant than the landscape spread out before his mind's eye was the din of remembered voices on his inner ear—South African voices talking incessantly about problems—problems of race, problems of language, and problems of separate living space. *Cry, the Beloved Country* is, in fact, a book for the ear rather than the eye. There are many works of art that incorporate a multitude of voices, from Greek tragedy, with its choruses comprising "the voices of the people," through Chaucer's many-voiced Prologue to the *Canterbury Tales*, to the multitude of voices in James Joyce's *Ulysses* and his medley of tongues in *Finnegans Wake*. What all these have in common is their mingled lyric and dramatic method; for a multitude of voices cannot be incorporated in discursive prose. Paton, then, did not superimpose a poetic, or lyrical, prose style on the social theme of his novel; rather he composed the novel of lyric and dramatic elements because, artistically, there was no other way to embody his powerfully felt emotion.

The essential interest in *Cry, the Beloved Country* lies in the compelling story that unfolds through the action of the plot; but three other artistic qualities combine to help make it an original and unique work of art: first, the poetic elements in the language of some of the characters; second, the lyric passages spoken from outside the action, like the well-known opening chapter; and third, the dramatic choral chapters that break the sequence of the story for social commentary, but nevertheless widen the horizons of the action to embrace the whole land. There are three such chapters, in particular: Chapter 9, a chorus of African voices; Chapter 12, a chorus of white voices; and Chapter 23, which is a mingled chorus on justice. In London editions this last is Book Two, Chapter 6.

The Chorus of African Voices, in Chapter 9, opens by picking up the refrain that first enters the novel in Chapter 2: "All roads lead to Johannesburg. If you are white or if you are black they lead to Johannesburg. If the crops fail there is work in Johannesburg." This choral chapter is composed of incremental snatches of anonymous dialogue, picked up, as it were, by roving television reporters. The chapter is therefore a collage of brief dramatic confrontations of Africans seeking places to live in the African townships of Alexandra, Sophiatown, or Orlando. These individual scenes are frequently interspersed with repetitions of this refrain, or variations on it:

> Have you a room to let?
> No, I have no room to let.
> Have you a room to let?
> It is let already.
> Have you a room to let?   (52)

The second choral episode, the Chorus of White Voices in Chapter 12, takes its rise from the incident in the preceding chapter where the clergy in the Mission House read of the murder of Arthur Jarvis. This choral chapter, which opens with the refrain, "Have no doubt there is fear in the land," specifically mentions a chorus of voices: "There are voices crying what must be done, a hundred thousand voices. . . . One cries this, and one cries that, and another cries something that is neither this nor that" (75). There are voices in this chorus demanding, for example, that crime be "stamped out," and other voices recommending that society be reformed—interchanges that lead to the event from which they generalize: "for the speaker of the evening, Mr. Arthur Jarvis, has just been shot dead in his house in Parkwold." At this point, a brief lyric passage that includes the refrain, "Cry, the beloved country, for the unborn child that is the inheritor of our fear; let him not love the earth too deeply," provides a bridge to the swirl of fear-filled activity as Kumalo and Msimangu search for Absalom.

Following Absolom's murder trial in Chapter 22 the focus of interest widens to a general consideration of social justice in Chapter 23—the final choral episode which centers on an actual event of 1946 in South Africa: the discovery of new rich gold deposits at Odendaalsrust in the Orange Free State, an event that occurred about the time of the novel's setting. So the trial scene, which opens with a commentary on justice under the law, is generalized: "There is little attention being paid to the trial of those accused of the murder of Arthur Jarvis of Parkwold. For gold has been discovered, more gold, rich gold" (167). In this chapter Paton employs an uncharacteristic degree of satire, aimed chiefly at the commercial community of primarily English-speaking adherents of the United party, then in power in South Africa.

While these choral scenes interrupt the flow of the plot in some degree, they do so to its advantage. Through them the reader gains an immediate perspective on the complex South African social system forming the background against which the plot is played out.

The Stages of Kumalo's Quest

The plot of *Cry, the Beloved Country* combines three related quests corresponding largely to Book One, Book Two, and Book Three of the work itself. Book One, the Book of Kumalo, is concerned at first with the physical quest of the Reverend Stephen Kumalo, who travels from the African village of Ndotsheni to Johannesburg in search of his sister Gertrude, his son Absalom, and his brother John, who have all "disappeared" in the metropolis. His guide to these regions of lost people is another Anglican priest, a fellow Zulu of wholly different background, the Reverend Theophilus Msimangu. Msimangu, as has been pointed out, is a man with a deep philosophic bent and clear logical mind whose secular hero was the sharp-witted philosopher Alfred Hoernlé. He guides Kumalo down among the lost people as Virgil guided Dante through the infernal regions, opening his eyes and his understanding to the meaning of enigmatic things. They find Stephen's sister Gertrude, his brother John, and, finally, his son Absalom, only to discover that he is the confessed murderer of Arthur Jarvis.

Book Two is the Book of James Jarvis, father of the murdered man. He sets out from the closed mental world of his own habitual assumptions and prejudices and seeks to understand the liberal spirit revealed to him in his son's reputation and writings. Again, on the analogy of Virgil led by Dante, James Jarvis, "seeking his way out of the fog into which he has been born," is guided by the voice of his dead son who had "journeyed . . . into strange waters" and set down his philosophy in "A Private Essay on the Evolution of a South African."

Book Three is the Book of Restoration. In it, the physical and psychological quests of the earlier books turn toward the spiritual path of redemption. This is the region where, after guiding him through the horrors of hell and the mount of purgatory, Virgil left Dante to proceed alone with no guide but love.

In Book One, Stephen Kumalo journeys to Johannesburg and experiences manifestations of good and evil in this strange new industrial world. He is robbed, and he is treated with kindness; he visits places of despair like Claremont where he finds his sister Gertrude, and places of hope like Ezenzeleni where the blind are rehabilitated; he witnesses his brother John's self-seeking corruption and Msimangu's selfless dedication; he becomes aware, too, of conflicting good and evil impulses within himself. He is a good man seeking lost sheep, yet he lies to his fellow-passengers on the train to protect his self-esteem; and he is cruel to the nameless girl who is to bear Absalom's child, as he is later cruel to his brother John whose cunning has saved his own son at Absalom's expense.

In Book Two the reader observes James Jarvis's deep experience as he returns again and again to the writings on social justice left by his murdered son. These papers argue the case for racial conciliation in South Africa from the Christian and liberal standpoint that Paton shared with Jan Hofmeyr. They open James Jarvis's eyes for the first time to the real plight of both rural and urban Africans—the destruction of their tribal social organization without provision for its replacement by something better: "It was permissible to allow the destruction of a tribal system that impeded the growth of the country. . . . But it is not permissible to watch its destruction, and to replace it by nothing, or by so little, that a whole people degenerates, physically and morally." They also open his eyes to the need for restitution and restoration: "Our civilization has therefore an inescapable duty to set up another system of order and tradition and convention . . ." (146).

The writings of his son's hero, Abraham Lincoln, guide James Jarvis in deciding the form the memorial to his dead son should take, for he returns more than once to the Gettysburg Address, in which he encounters: "It is rather for us to be here dedicated to the great task remaining before us—that from these honored dead we take increased devotion to that cause for which they gave the last full measure of devotion; that we here highly resolve that these dead shall not have died in vain. . . ."[5]

James Jarvis realizes that his son had journeyed into deep waters, but he also realizes that he must honor and carry forward his son's work as far as it is possible for him to do so. He is not equipped to do his son's work, but he does "the next best thing." He therefore gives practical financial help to the African Boys' Club and to the drought-stricken village of Ndotsheni. And he learns to respect the sufferings of the old man whose son had murdered his son.

Book Three: Restoration

The theme of restoration pervades Book Three on several levels. There is a beginning made on the restoration of the land through the work of a young agricultural demonstrator; there is the restoration of Kumalo's leaky village church through the generosity of James Jarvis; and this, in turn, is a halting step towards the restoration of brotherhood—one human being reaching out toward another across the barriers of fear and prejudice. The climax of the theme of spiritual restoration is reached when Kumalo, who in Book One neared despair, makes his lone pilgrimage to the mountaintop to share his son's agony on the morning set for his execution.

Book Three, seeking to evoke a Christian sensibility, may be open to the dual danger of uncritical applause from those who share Paton's faith, and to charges of sentimentality from those who do not. Yet Paton does not permit the reader either to applaud Jarvis's "conversion" or to smile tolerantly on it as a matter beyond the limits of

practical sociological concern. At this very point in the novel he quite
deliberately raises the question: "What courses of action are the
concern of a practical man, and what courses of action are impractical?" His answer ironically contrasts two ways of undertaking the
relief of present suffering.

One way is to hope for an ideal, utopian solution through the
intervention of some agent of authority or impersonal force, such as
the state, equipped with blueprints and long-range theories. Another
way is, meanwhile, to do "the next best thing" and take those
practical steps, however small, that lie within reach. The "good"
characters in the novel do not accept evils passively. They act, not
only for "humanitarian" reasons, but because as human beings they
are involved in mankind, and are in a real sense their brothers'
keepers. It is, indeed, a simple personal action—an assumption of the
responsibility of priestly brotherhood that opens up the whole Pando-
ra's box: namely, Msimangu's letter to Kumalo informing him of his
sister Gertrude's "sickness." Kumalo learns in Johannesburg that he,
too, bears a measure of personal responsibility for alleviating suffering; and must *act* like Msimangu, and the people at Ezenzeleni and
the reformatory, and like Dubula who set up Shanty Town. He
decides on the unprecedented, if unrewarding, step of seeking an
interview with the chief to propose some practical steps to alleviate
the suffering caused in Ndotsheni by the drought. And he does this
because "the great city had opened his eyes to something that had
been begun and must now be continued."

Next he seeks out the headmaster of the local school, where, as the
chief reminded him, "we have been teaching these things for many
years." There is a fine irony in Paton's portrait of the headmaster that
satirizes the impracticality of theoretical schemes. Paton even employs a singsong rhythm—like those who parrot, by rote, things
uncomprehended—that mocks the headmaster: "his office was filled
with notices in blue and red and green." When Kumalo sought his
advice about practical measures, he was answered in theoretical
educational jargon pitifully far removed from reality: "The headmaster explained that the school was trying to relate the life of the child to
the life of the community, and showed him circulars from the Department in Pietermaritzburg, all about these matters. He took Kumalo

out into the blazing sun, and showed him the school gardens, but this was an academic lecture, for there was no water, and everything was dead" (233). It is against this background of futile, high-sounding schemes and theories that Jarvis's simple, practical act of providing milk for the sick children is set with purposeful, yet profound, irony. For it was not only because of the drought that "there was no water, and everything was dead"; but, symbolically, because the schemes and theories themselves were arid. It is only when Jarvis and Kumalo meet humbly as two human beings, each aware of the weight of the other's suffering, and therefore of their common humanity, that the drought breaks and the rain comes at last to the valley of Ndotsheni.

Paton's *Cry, the Beloved Country* offers no blueprint for a utopian society. It offers instead recognition of personal responsibility. The crucial development in the characters of both Jarvis and Kumalo is that each comes to recognize how individual fear or indifference infects society with moral paralysis; and that the antidote for this paralysis is individual courage willing to go forward in faith. They do not wait, therefore, for some miraculous healing of this paralysis to be brought about by the direct intervention of God, or through the implementation of some scheme for a final solution, or through the flowering of the promises of some manifesto. They act by taking whatever steps are possible to them as individuals in the immediate present. A road taken in faith has no certainty of arrival; if it did, faith would be unnecessary. *Cry, the Beloved Country*, therefore, rightly concludes with an acceptance of uncertainty: "But when the dawn will come of our emancipation, from the fear of bondage and the bondage of fear, why, that is a secret" (277).

Chapter Four

The Pride of Pure Race:
Too Late the Phalarope

Afrikaner Nationalism and World War II

The note of hope in *Cry, the Beloved Country* had some real basis in fact. There were signs in the months immediately following World War II that South African society was prepared to accept new departures in race relations. In 1946 Prime Minister J. C. Smuts had appointed a commission to look into South Africa's urban conditions and the problems of migratory African labor—the very conditions and problems that impelled Paton to write *Cry, the Beloved Country*. It was generally expected that this commission, known as the Fagan Commission, would present liberal recommendations to Parliament. It was also generally anticipated that any such recommendations would be implemented by Parliament through the influence of Deputy Prime Minister Jan Hofmeyr, who then seemed likely to succeed General Smuts as Prime Minister.

In 1948, the year *Cry, the Beloved Country* appeared, the typical rhythm of white South African politics reasserted itself. Any suspicion that the Liberal Spirit is working among parliamentary leaders starts a groundswell for racial intolerance among conservative white voters, particularly in rural areas. In the general elections of that year, Dr. Malan's Nationalist Party received an unexpectedly large plurality for its policy of *apartheid* that denied Africans the right to permanent residence in the urban areas of "white" South Africa, and emphasized ineradicable cultural differences between their tribal heritage and the heritage of "Western Civilization," which is thought to be the birthright of whites only. Jan Hofmeyr died a few months after this election, and with him went much of the hope of powerful, outspoken Parliamentary opposition to the new government's *apart-*

heid policies. In these respects the hope of going forward in faith implicitly present in *Cry, the Beloved Country* was diminished.

By 1952, the year that Paton wrote *Too Late the Phalarope* during a three-month period in London and Cornwall, the South African government had begun implementing *apartheid* with little regard for opposition views. But Paton did not set his new novel with any obviousness in the post-1948 period; for his purpose was not simply to describe *apartheid*, but to explore the racial attitudes that gave rise to it. He is not concerned, therefore, in this novel with immediate social and economic manifestations of *apartheid* that followed the 1948 election. Instead he probed into its ideological roots in the doctrine of Pure Race; and into the extent to which this racial ideal—placed above all other considerations—constituted a false deity, or "heretical Christianity," as he calls it elsewhere. It is this pride in Pure Race, set up as a religious doctrine, that the narrator, Tante Sophie, has in mind in her summing up: "I pray we shall not walk arrogant, remembering Herod whom an Angel of the Lord struck down for that he made himself God" (272). Sophie's view of racial arrogance has affinities with the Greek concept of *hubris*—the special manifestation of pride that incurs tragic retribution. *Hubris* is the arrogation by mortals of attributes proper only to the immortal gods, and tragedy is the inevitable destruction meted out to *hubris*.

Too Late the Phalarope tells the story of Pieter van Vlaanderen, a young police lieutenant decorated in war and also nationally famous as a rugby football player. He is a married man with two children, highly respected in the rural Afrikaner community and, indeed, the kind of man in whose presence other men feel constrained to subdue loud talk or off-color jokes. Yet Pieter van Vlaanderen transgresses the strict prohibitions of the South African Immorality Act, which forbids sexual relations between members of different races, and thereby brings tragic destruction on himself and his family. This novel of van Vlaanderen's tragic downfall differs greatly in fictional method from its predecessor, *Cry, the Beloved Country*. In the first place it concentrates on the inner struggles in the soul of one man, and for the clamor of many voices and the broad overview of South Africa, it substitutes an inner dialogue between two aspects of a divided personality. Furthermore, while the theme of restoration is still fundamental in this second novel, it is approached indirectly, and its attendant note of hope is muted.

Too Late the Phalarope is set in a small town in the eastern Trans-vaal—a district populated almost wholly by Afrikaans-speaking white farmers who cherish the four fundamental and inseparable tenets of Afrikaner Nationalism: *Volk, Kerk, Taal, Land* ("people, church, language, soil"). The *Volk* is the separate and unique Afrikaner People descended from the Voortrekkers; the *Kerk* is the Afrikaner branch of the Dutch Reformed Church to which, ideally, all the *Volk* adhere; the *Taal* is the Afrikaans language, which, in place of a national boundary, identifies their nationhood; and the *Land* is the soil of South Africa, sacred to the Afrikaner *Volk* in almost the same sense that the Promised Land was sacred to the Israelites.

These fundamental ideals are trenchantly summed up in *Too Late the Phalarope* by the Afrikaner patriarch, old Jakob van Vlaanderen, when he rebukes his drunken guest, Flip van Vuuren, who persisted in demanding, "What's the point of living, what's the point of life?": "So Jakob van Vlaanderen stood up from his chair, and said in a voice of thunder, the point of living is to serve the Lord your God, and to uphold the honour of your church and language and people, take him home" (92). Jakob van Vlaanderen represents the attitude of those Afrikaans-speaking South Africans who refused to accept Louis Botha's ideal of bringing all white South Africans together in a common patriotism. His wife and his sister, Tante Sophie, adhere to Louis Botha's ideal of union among Afrikaans-speaking and English-speaking whites; his son Pieter, in the finer aspects of his character, might be said to personify Botha's ideal.

One of the causes of friction between Jakob and his son Pieter is the difference in their estimates of where the duties of patriotism lie. At the outbreak of World War II in 1939, the South African Parliament was divided on the question of entering the war against Hitler's Germany on Britain's side, or remaining neutral; and General Smuts carried his motion for participation by a very narrow majority. The white population at large was similarly divided. So it was found expedient to agree that men already in the armed forces and police should be permitted either to retain their positions at home or to volunteer for service abroad. Those who so volunteered were identified by orange tabs worn on the shoulder-straps of their uniform tunics, which distinguished them from those who did not take the oath. The oath taken by these volunteers came to be known as "the red oath" from the color of the tabs. Jakob van Vlaanderen was one of those who saw the war as "an English war" in which no true Afrikaner should participate: "And when his son Pieter took the red oath and had gone to war, he would bear no mention of his name. . . ." When Pieter returned, Jakob would refer to his service medals and decorations, which included the Distinguished Service Order, as "foreign trash."

Pieter's volunteering for war service was later to play a large part in his tragic downfall. Since he had attained the rank of major in the wartime army, he returned, in peacetime, to the local police force as an officer. He therefore outranked Sergeant Steyn, who had more seniority but who, sharing Jakob's Afrikaner patriotism, had refused to take "the red oath." This is the source of the enmity that makes Sergeant Steyn the instrument of Pieter's destruction. Steyn is something of an Iago, but his hatred is not motiveless. As *Cry, the Beloved Country* embodied an authentic portrait of one aspect of urban African life in South Africa in 1946, so *Too Late the Phalarope* embodies an authentic portrait of one aspect of Afrikaner Nationalism on the eve of its political triumph in 1948.

Historical Realism

As he did in *Cry, the Beloved Country*, and later in *Ah, But Your Land Is Beautiful*, Paton achieved a sense of authenticity in his second novel by weaving certain actual events of the time into the action of his plot. In his hands these actual events become dramatic properties inseparable from the action of the story.

One of these "properties" is the book that Lieutenant Pieter van Vlaanderen gives as a birthday gift to his father. The nonfictional model for this fictional book was *The Birds of South Africa*—a comprehensive work with fine color illustrations like the Audubon series in the United States, published in a new edition in South Africa in 1948. [1] For Paton, one of whose hobbies is bird-watching, this would have been a memorable event, made even more memorable by the fact

that its author, the respected naturalist Austin Roberts, died that
year. The title of this book pleases old Jakob van Vlaanderen, to
whom the name South Africa borders on the sacred. But the name of
the author repels him. He will not even mention it, and he always
refers to the author as "the Englishman." Since Paton does not reveal
the author's name, readers are left to assume that old Jakob's repugnance is a measure of his hostility to Englishmen in general. But there
would be good reason for Jakob's special repugnance toward the name
Roberts, for the British general whose armies invaded the Transvaal
across the very terrain of the novel's setting, and who for a time during
the Boer War virtually ruled South Africa, was General Lord Roberts.
(When the Nationalist party came to power in 1948 they changed the
name of South Africa's main military base at Pretoria from Roberts
Heights to Voortrekkerhoogte, i.e., Voortrekker Heights.)

It may be the touch of obscurity resulting from Paton's reluctance
to extend to his readers a clearer motive for Jakob's repugnance toward
its author that leads some to seek symbolic significance in the book of
birds and, in particular, in the elusive little wading bird, the phalarope. The book of birds does affect the relations between Jakob and his
son, but it is not a symbol in any exact sense. Neither is the phalarope
a symbol. It is an actual bird about whose habits old Jakob, in fact,
knew more than "the Englishman" who wrote the book. In *The Birds
of South Africa*, Austin Roberts has some hesitation in classifying the
phalarope as a South African bird, because he has only one recorded
observation of each of the two species of phalarope, the "Grey" and the
"Red-necked," on South African coasts. Jakob knew the phalarope as
a fairly common inland bird also, and the Englishman's ignorance was
a topic, therefore, that he was happy to discuss even with his son
Pieter, with whom he had never before achieved rapport.

Another actual event of the period—or an account closely based on
it—helps Paton to establish the atmosphere of obsession with racial
purity in a society where the most unforgivable thing is to break "the
iron law that no white man might touch a black woman"; and that the
most terrible thing in the world is to have such a transgression
discovered. This is the case of "the man Smith," modeled on an actual
contemporary case of a white farmer who murdered a servant girl who
was pregnant by him. In the hope of preventing the discovery of his

victim's identity, which might lead to his own discovery, "the man Smith," with his wife's complicity, cut off and hid the murdered girl's head. In Paton's account, this gruesome crime by an otherwise mild-mannered man is interpreted principally as a consequence of his fear that his illicit sexual relations across the racial line would be discovered.

The Sin against the Race

This account of "the man Smith" provides a dramatic instance of the general air of intense concern with the issue of race mixture that followed the Nationalist party election victory of 1948. There was then a law in force against illicit sexual relations between white and nonwhite. This was Act 5 of 1927, under which Lieutenant Pieter van Vlaanderen is charged in the novel *Too Late the Phalarope*. In 1949 and 1950 there were further extensions of this basic law: the Prohibition of Mixed Marriages Act of 1949, and the Immorality Act Amendment Act of 1950. The basic law may at one time have had the merit its supporters claimed for it of protecting African women from the whims of white overlords, but the extensions of the basic act reveal the essence of the new Nationalist ideal. By prohibiting interracial marriage even at a church ceremony, and by extending the act to cover any racial mixing—as, for example, between the white and Indian or Cape Colored communities—the emphasis is clearly focused on the ideal of Pure Race, and not on the protection of vulnerable women. One may find interesting corroboration of this attitude in textbooks widely used in Transvaal schools in the 1950s. In the chapter "Race Relations: White and non-White" in a junior high-school textbook in social studies, there is a section subheaded "The Sin of Race Mixture" which argues that God wills separate races. This section culminates in a long quotation from someone identified only as "one of our great statesmen" that begins with what is tantamount to a summary of *Too Late the Phalarope*: "We must all keep our people white. Great is the pain for blood-relatives and friends if anyone sins against this highest law; greater still is the scandal when a people sins against its own blood."[2]

It is within this context of an ideal of racial purity that regarded race mixture as the ultimate sin—the sin "against this highest law," as the school textbook puts it—that Paton sets the tragedy of Pieter van Vlaanderen. Various characters in *Too Late the Phalarope* embody contrasting attitudes to this sin against the highest law. Some, representing a majority view in the town of Venterspan, uphold the law with iron determination. These include Pieter's father, old Jakob van Vlaanderen, and his father-in-law, who declares he would shoot the offender like a dog. The proponents of this kind of justice also include his fellow policeman Sergeant Steyn and the previously admiring young recruit Vorster. Others view Pieter's transgression with greater compassion, but these are a minority, represented by his aunt, Tante Sophie; his mother; the English-speaking police officer Captain Massingham; and the Jewish storekeeper Matthew Kaplan, who is affectionately known by the Afrikaans diminutive "Kappie." It is chiefly through the contrasting attitudes of old Jakob and Tante Sophie that we see the opposing themes of destruction and restoration brought into confrontation; and here the sacrificial justice demanded by the iron law outweighs the compassionate justice exhorted by Christ to his followers. Ironically, this victory of vengence over compassion is exactly what the novel propounds as the greatest of all offenses from a Christian standpoint. Pieter's superior officer, Captain Massingham, sums this up when he says: "An offender must be punished, *mejuffrou*, I don't argue about that. But to punish and not to restore, that is the greatest of all offences." And Tante Sophie, significantly, responds, "Is that the sin against the Holy Ghost?"(292).

These contrasting attitudes, pitting the demand for utter destruction of the wrongdoer against the impulse toward forgiveness and restoration, bear significantly on one's perception of *Too Late the Phalarope* as a tragedy in the literary sense. It may be useful, therefore, to look more closely at Jakob and Sophie, the two chief embodiments of these attitudes.

Judgment or Mercy

Jakob van Vlaanderen, as his name suggests, combines some of the qualities of an Old Testament patriarch with qualities derived from the Afrikaner's elemental Flemish roots. Enshrined in his Transvaal home is the great family Bible in the Dutch-language version, containing the names of the van Vlaanderens for 150 years. His forebears had brought it with them from the Cape Colony when they trekked inland in the 1830s to set up their independent Boer republics beyond the reach of British laws and their equal application to white and black. Jakob van Vlaanderen was a strong-willed giant of a man who understood the word obedience "better than he understood the word love." He was an upright man, just in accordance with his own unwavering principles. He believed that his duty to God demanded that he uphold the separateness and racial purity of the Afrikaner people. As befitted his exclusive nationalism, he was a lover of all things South African, including the birds of the veld.

Jakob understood strength and determination in a man, but not sensitivity; he treated the sensitive side of his son's character—his pleasure in such fragile beautiful things as flowers and stamps—with harshness and suspicion. Eventually, prompted by his son's gift of a book of South African birds, he took hesitant steps toward reconciliation. He arranged to show Pieter the phalarope, the little wading bird about whose habits the author of the book was mistaken; and, although perplexed by the whole thing, he even purchased some expensive stamps for him.

This thaw in the iciness of his attitude toward his son adds great poignancy to the novel by suggesting what might have been; but it is not the fact that father and son recognized a common interest too late that supplies the essential element of tragedy. An essential element in Greek tragedy, in addition to the flaw in the hero's character, is that the fate of those enmeshed in its web is determined, like that of King Oedipus, by a power outside their control. Such an external determining element is present in *Too Late the Phalarope* in the form of a fundamental assumption that the Afrikaner people are a Pure Race set apart. Therefore, when Jakob hears that his son has "sinned against the race," he knows exactly what his duty to the race demands of him: "So he took the pen and ink, and he crossed out the name of Pieter van Vlaanderen from the book. . . ." Then, referring to Pieter's gift of the book of birds: "You will take the book, he said, and the pipe, and everything that the man ever gave to me, and every likeness of him, and everything in this house that has anything to do with him, and you will burn and destroy them all" (251). This ritual of denial culminates in prayer to God for the destruction of his son's soul; for Jakob solemnly opened the family Bible and read "the most terrible words that man has ever written" from the Hundred and Ninth Psalm, beginning: *"When he shall be judged, let him be condemned; and let his prayer become sin."* And old Jakob read on, blind to the irony that "the most terrible words" of the psalm are explicitly directed against the man *"who remembered not to show mercy."*

Old Jakob's actions are predictable. The reader, in fact, accepts them as the inevitable expression of his character. But they are ultimately dictated by an impersonal force outside himself rather than by a father's response to a son's transgression. For Old Jakob could not act otherwise and still maintain the purity of race as the highest law.

By contrast, the qualities of mercy and compassion are embodied in Jakob's maiden sister, Tante Sophie van Vlaanderen, who relates Pieter's story. It seems likely that for the characterization of Sophie, Paton drew on his recollections of his own aunt, Elizabeth Paton; and, indeed, the complex relationships among members of the van Vlaanderen family—father, son, mother, and aunt—have parallels in Paton's family experience. His father was an autocrat quick to punish. This aroused rebelliousness in Paton and his brother; and their mother gave selfless devotion to both father and sons. Of his aunt Elizabeth who followed her brother to South Africa Paton says in *Towards the Mountain*:

She was a good and generous woman. For some reason she did not marry, and she poured out her affection on me, my brother Athol, and my sisters. . . . What caused her grief was that at least the three eldest children were afraid of their father; they resented his extreme authority and he came near to destroying their filial affection. (11)

In *Too Late the Phalarope* Sophie, who did not marry, is a watcher set apart from normal family life and love by a severe facial disfigurement. She has lived all her life at Jakob's house, and she has lavished on her young nephew, Pieter, all the affection of her own unfulfilled maternal instincts. We therefore see both father and son from her sympathetic viewpoint. Her concern for these men, and indeed for all men, is deeply Christian; her Christianity, based on love, contrasts strikingly with Jakob's narrower, puritanical Christianity that respects obedience above all. As narrator, Sophie presents the other characters in all their human frailty; but she refrains from passing judgment on them. She is at pains, for example, to show the human side of Jakob: "For some said he was a hard and loveless man, and would ride down any that stood in his way without pity or mercy. But I tell you it was not true." Yet she is not a party to Jakob's extreme devotion to exclusive Afrikaner nationalism; she prefers to retain her allegiance to Louis Botha's policy of reconciliation.

Sophie has other advantages as a narrator besides her magnanimity of outlook. Having lived all her life with the van Vlaanderen family, she can link her knowledge of Pieter's childhood relations with his father to the events of his tragedy. She recognizes that his downfall is not brought about wholly by momentary temptation, but that it is a consequence of accumulated life experience. Her ability to reveal how past events foreshadowed destruction intensifies the element of tragic inevitability in the novel.

Although Sophie is an observer set aside, with little power over events, she is emotionally involved in the fortunes of Pieter and Jakob. This appears to be one of Paton's main motives in creating her. Speaking of the vitality of the South African novel in English, particularly in the hands of writers of English or Jewish extraction, or Colored writers like Peter Abrahams, Paton has remarked that in South Africa, where the racial struggle primarily pits African against Afrikaner: "It is the Englishman, the Jew and the Coloured man, who are, even when they are drawn into the struggle, the observers. It is they who are better placed than either Afrikaner or African . . . to see the real drama that history has unfolded, even when they are deeply or emotionally involved."[3]

In *Too Late the Phalarope*, Tante Sophie fills an analogous role. She is presented to us as someone consciously aware of her own powers of observation. She knows that she developed these powers because she was set apart from the ordinary stream of life by her disfigurement: "I have learned to know the meaning of unnoticed things, of a pulse that beats suddenly, of a glance that moves from here to there. . . ." It was she who rightly suspected the marital difficulties between Pieter and his wife Nella; it was she who correctly interpreted Stephanie's sensual invitation to Pieter; it was she who felt uncomfortable about the flirtatious Cousin Anna, who wore the yellow trousers. Paton's device of the secret diary as one source of her information may be an arbitrary one, but it proves useful in establishing her reliability as an observer; for, at key points, she is able to quote from the diary to confirm her original intuition.[4]

Whatever her technical limitations, one must admit that only a narrator of Tante Sophie's qualities of mind could provide a suitable vehicle for the religious theme of the novel: namely, that it is not the judgment of God but the judgment of men that is a stranger to compassion.

The Way of Temptation

The plot of *Too Late the Phalarope* has two complementary movements. In the first the events leading to Pieter van Vlaanderen's temptation and sin gradually unfold; in the second he becomes increasingly enmeshed in a web of tragedy and destruction. Chapters 1 through 19 may be said, therefore, to comprise the Book of Temptation; Chapters 20 through 39, the Book of Retribution. The two complementary actions imply an ironic contrast; namely, that even though Pieter's adultery transgresses the laws of God, it is not God, but an idol—the false deity of Pure Race—that exacts the terrible retribution of Pieter's destruction, and the destruction of all belonging to him.

In the first movement, here termed the Book of Temptation, Paton represents Pieter van Vlaanderen's temptation and sin as arising from several interrelated causes. One cause is psychological. Pieter is aware of two conflicting sides to his character: the one, brave and upright; the other possessed by an elemental urge attracting him, he says, to what he most hated. He conceals this side of his character behind a mask of cold reserve, and when this urge takes hold of him he calls it "the mad sickness." Evidently this "mad sickness" is a strong, but unwanted, sexual attraction to women outside his marriage. His comment on his father's simple, matter-of-fact statement that he had never touched a woman other than his wife is: "I felt . . . a feeling of envy too, and wonder that I was otherwise." Since Pieter also envies those fellow students at the university who spoke of their physical revulsion to the touch of a nonwhite person—a revulsion he does not share—it seems clear that by "the mad sickness" he means a sexual desire forbidden by the iron law of his people "that no black woman should be touched by a white man."

The novel suggests that the psychological conflict in Pieter's character has roots in his childhood relations with his father. Referring to his father's anger at his interest in stamp collecting, Pieter says bitterly to Matthew Kaplan: "There was trouble long before the stamps . . . I was born before the stamps." In this respect Pieter's desire for Stephanie can be rationalized as an impulse to revolt against all his father stood for. But Paton does not rationalize Pieter's action to the extent of lifting the burden of responsibility from his shoulders and transferring it to old Jakob. Pieter was conscious of his problem, and could have sought help. Indeed, his successive attempts to reveal himself to the young clergyman, Dominee Vos, to Kappie, and to Captain Massingham, constitute one link between the theme of temptation, which he can choose to resist, and the web of tragedy manipulated by forces outside his power. There is tragic irony in his successive failures to unburden himself. On each occasion that he attempts to do so, the regard in which others hold him—their worshipful attitude toward him as their hero—intervenes. Even though he had but one thought in his mind—"to tell one human soul of the misery of my life, that I was tempted by what I hated"—a fatal flaw prevents him from doing so; and he asks, but leaves unanswered, "Was it pride that prevented me?"

Another source of Pieter's inner conflict is the tension between him and his wife Nella, arising from her somewhat prudish attitude to married love. In her marriage, Sophie tells us, Nella had "some idea that was good and true but twisted in some small place, that the love of the body, though good and true, was apart from the love of the soul." Nella's "twisted" attitude to married love may be, partly, a heritage from the religious Puritanism of her people; but her extreme revulsion at hearing that the boy Dick had attempted to accost the black girl, Stephanie, suggests that her other heritage, the ideal of Pure Race, is inextricably entwined with her religious outlook. If so, the characterization of Nella provides, like Book Three of *Cry, the Beloved Country*, and a number of themes in *Towards the Mountain*, yet another instance of Paton's distrust of convictions that substitute an inhuman perfection for the flesh and blood realities of the human condition.

If Nella's part in Pieter's susceptibility to temptation is remote, the part played by Anna is immediate and physical. Anna occupies Tante Sophie's thoughts to a surprising extent—wholly out of proportion to her two brief appearances in the novel. Anna, who is described as "a kind of cousin," works in the city and has acquired city attitudes toward fashions in dress and social drinking. Not really wicked, Anna is flashy, bored by the small town, and slightly vulgar. She is, ultimately, the temptress who, partly unwittingly, is the immediate instrument of Pieter's destruction. At the critical psychological moment when his black mood is deepest as a combined consequence of Nella's obtuse letter, Sergeant Steyn's mistake, and the high emotional temperature that caused him to write his letter of resignation, Anna waylays him with feminine wiles and the plea "I'm dying for a drink." So, in the Royal Hotel, they have brandy after brandy, "more than he had ever drunk before." Aroused by the brandies, Anna's company, and her parting kiss, he goes to meet Stephanie in the vacant ground. Paton implies, nevertheless, that Pieter's choice is deliberate; for whatever force the underlying psychological drives, the brandies, and Anna's company may have released, his final preparations for the encounter with Stephanie are calculated.

In contrast to Pieter's agonizing struggles, the black girl Stephanie has a simple, uncomplicated purpose for seeking him out. Her life in and out of prison for the repeated offence of brewing illicit liquor, is devoted to the single-minded aim of retaining the sole object of her love—her illegitimate child. In her instinctive preoccupation with the safety of her child, she seizes on the only possibility she can think of for recruiting this great man's protection; it is for the same reason—to avert danger to her child—that she later carries out Sergeant Steyn's plan to destroy him.

Retribution and Tragedy

The second movement of the plot of *Too Late the Phalarope*, the Book of Retribution, reaches beyond the psychological and moral aspects of temptation toward the pity and terror of tragedy. First, however, we should note how easily Paton solves a literary problem some critics have declared to be insurmountable: that of reconciling a Christian viewpoint with tragedy as a literary form. Paton undercuts the dilemma by building his tragedy, not on the consequences of Pieter van Vlaanderen's act understood as a sin against God (he leaves this as an inner, private matter), but on the consequences of his act understood as a "sin against the race." He therefore disposes of the matter of the sin against God's law in a single paragraph, in which Pieter prays to God, partly for forgiveness for his act and partly for forgiveness for presuming to pray at such a moment. This short paragraph closes with a striking metaphor for the theological assertion that sin cuts man off from God:

For he had a vision that a trumpet had been blown in Heaven, and that the Lord Most High had ordered the closing of the doors, that no prayer might enter in from such a man, who knowing the laws and the commandments, had, of his own choice and will, defied them. (154)

From this point on, Paton's literary concern is not with Pieter's guilt but with his terror of discovery. For even while Pieter was praying he heard a twig crack, and he suspected a watcher in the dark. Thereafter he prays repeatedly, not for forgiveness, but that he might not be discovered. Paton builds up Pieter's mounting terror in great detail, for only by demonstrating the intensity of the tragic character's terror of the impending evil can he assure the reader that the tragic blow, when it comes, is tantamount to total annihilation. But the blow does not fall on Pieter immediately, and for a time he feels assured that his prayers to avoid discovery have been answered. Therefore when the blow does fall, it comes suddenly and from an unexpected quarter. The events he interpreted as signs that his transgression had been discovered turn out to be either mere coincidence or the shallow practical jokes of the welfare worker Japie Grobler. Pieter's endurance of terror brings a full recognition that the consequences of his act, if discovered, will involve not only himself but Nella and his children and all who bore the name van Vlaanderen. There is hope that his determination to avoid bringing destruction on them will strengthen him against the desire for Stephanie.

These glimmerings of hope seem to point toward a new dawn when old Jakob arranges the family picnic where he and Pieter watch for the phalarope together. But the growing inner determination, the picnic, and the phalarope come too late. Sergeant Steyn, like Iago in his enmity, takes a hint of suspicion for surety. He sets a trap for Pieter. And out of fear for the security of her child, Stephanie carries out Steyn's purpose. She plants the evidence on Pieter and turns witness against him, and he is convicted and sentenced to prison for contravening the Immorality Act, No. 5 of 1927.

Restoration

After his conviction, Pieter's destruction as a public man is complete and more enduring than his prison sentence. As he had once explained to young Dick: "It's a thing that's never forgiven, never forgotten. The court may give you a year, two years. But outside it's a sentence for life." In the society that made the iron laws there is no hope of public forgiveness or restoration. The characters representing the forces of arrogant pride in race treat the transgressor with contempt. Therefore, in *Too Late the Phalarope*, as in *Cry, the Beloved Country*, the theme of restoration centers on the characters, representing the forces of love, who try in their various ways to restore Pieter. His friend Kappie, the Jewish storekeeper, suffers mutely with him, but acts with courage to dissuade him from suicide. Captain Massingham is able to put the theme of restoration into words. It is he who recognizes that to destroy and not to restore is the greatest of all offences, and it is his words that make Sophie understand that Pieter's future rests with Nella, the injured wife: "There is a hard law, *mejouffrou*, that when a deep injury is done to us we never recover until we forgive" (266). The most meaningful forgiveness must come from Nella, for she is the person most wronged by Pieter's action.

As Sergeant Steyn's hatred was an agent of Pieter's destruction, his mother's love is the agent of the measure of restoration possible to him. Sophie attributes Nella's return to stand by Pieter during his trial to the agency of his mother's love: "the girl came back, silent but steadfast, borne on the strong deep river of the mother's love."

The depth of selfless love manifested in Pieter's mother contrasts with the devotion of others to pride in Pure Race. We learn little of her in the novel beyond Sophie's estimate that "if ever a woman was all love, it was she . . ." (4). Her unselfish love is set as a healing spring in the desert of destructive racial pride. Significantly, in her personal relations with people and her humanitarian concern for the welfare of others less fortunate, she provides another fictional parallel for the qualities of Edith Rheinallt Jones that Paton describes in "A Deep Experience." Sophie's final summing up suggests this when she says that Pieter's story would be better told by her sister: "And I wish she could have written it, for maybe of the power of her love that never sought itself, men would have turned to the holy task of pardon, that the body of the Lord might not be wounded twice, and virtue come of our offences" (272).

In the thirty years since the writing of *Too Late the Phalarope* the terror of detection—or the destruction attendant on it —has not lessened for those found in violation of the Immorality Act of 1927 as amended in 1950. Writing of present circumstances in 1980 in *Towards the Mountain*, Paton says of the consequences of this law:

The great majority of the men who break this law are white. If a white man of any substance, a minister of religion, a lawyer, a schoolmaster, is found guilty of breaking this law, his life is ruined, even if the court suspends the punishment. At the time I write this, three white men have committed suicide in the last few weeks rather than face trial. More and more white people are asking themselves which is the greater offence, to commit a sin of the flesh or to destroy the person who commits it. (*TM*, 16)

Jakob van Vlaanderen and his kind do not ask themselves such questions.

Chapter Five

Short Fiction: The Diepkloof Stories and the Play *Sponono*

No Ivory Tower

Almost thirty years were to pass between Paton's writing of *Too Late the Phalarope* in Cornwall in 1952 and the publication of his third novel, *Ah, But Your Land Is Beautiful* in 1981. A large proportion of what he wrote in the interim was devoted to the political cause of the Liberal party of South Africa and its program for a nonracial society. Much of this writing was polemical, and in some degree ephemeral, including, for instance, his regular column "The Long View" in the Liberal party newspaper, *Contact*, and two pamphlets, in particular, on the forced removal of black families from land they had long owned in areas designated "white" by the Group Areas Act of 1950: *The People Wept: Being a Brief Account of . . . That Unjust Law . . . Known as The Group Areas Act of 1950* (1958), and *The Charlestown Story* (1960). But Paton also completed a number of major nonfictional works of more permanent interest during this thirty-year period. These included his two biographies, *A South African Tragedy: The Life and Times of Jan Hofmeyr* (1965) and *Apartheid and the Archbishop: The Life and Times of Geoffrey Clayton* (1973), and also two autobiographical volumes, *For You Departed* (1969) and *Towards the Mountain* (1980).

Between 1948 when he resigned from Diepkloof and 1953 when he began to work for the Liberal party, Paton produced a small body of short fiction and verse to which he added from time to time in subsequent years. Most of this short fiction was collected in *Tales from a Troubled Land* (published in England under the variant title *Debbie Go Home*)[1]; and some verse and additional fiction was later collected in *Knocking on the Door* (1975).

There is a quality of ambivalence in Paton's short fiction and verse of this period—as if he felt a tension between the claims of personal and public themes—such as might be felt by someone wishing to withdraw to the secluded garden of philosophy who is urgently being called on to help with some public catastrophe. Personal themes occupy him, for example, in such verse as "Meditation for a Young Boy Confirmed" and "To a Small Boy Who Died at Diepkloof Reformatory," both written in 1949 and collected in *Knocking on the Door* (1975). The personal element is also evident in a group of stories derived from experiences at Diepkloof Reformatory that constitute about half of the collection, *Tales from a Troubled Land*. Such personal fiction does not necessarily lack either interest or excellence; but it clearly differs from *l'art engage*—a category into which other stories in *Tales from a Troubled Land* unquestionably fall; stories in this second group reflect a painful vision of the cruel human degradation often attendant upon communal, racial, or ideological hate. The more personal Diepkloff stories were the earliest written. The first of them, "The Worst Thing of His Life," was published in 1951. It seems appropriate, therefore, in approaching Paton's short fiction to speak first of this group of stories and their relationship to the Play, *Sponono*, derived from three of them by Krishna Shah.

The Diepkloof Stories

Six of the ten stories in Paton's collection *Tales from a Troubled Land* are set in Diepkloof Reformatory. Two of them, "The Worst Thing of His Life" and "The Elephant Shooter," are little more than vignettes that present engaging portraits of white Afrikaner members of the reformatory staff. (Paton also writes appreciatively of a number of these young Afrikaners on his staff in his autobiography *Towards the Mountain*.) The remaining four Diepkloof stories are more elaborate psychological studies of young African inmates. The Principal, who appears as narrator in all of them, is not presented in a particularly good light, for they are all stories of his failures, or, at best, of his limited successes. The stories in this group are uneven. Two or three of them, even though they illustrate some universal theme like the human need for recognition of worth, are more in the nature of incidents than plotted fiction with organic development. Some reviewers of the *Tales from a Troubled Land*, including Edward Weeks in the *Atlantic*, selected "Death of a Tsotsi" as the best of them. The name *tsotsi* (pronounced tzu-tzi) was given to members of juvenile African gangs in the early 1950s. The word *tsotsi* is an African corruption of the American term "zoot suit." The zoot suit was a forerunner of the leather jackets, or any similar fashion in clothing associated with youthful gangs in cities anywhere. Spike, the chief character in "Death of a Tsotsi," liked flashy clothing; and even in the reformatory he livened up his uniform by wearing a red scarf on all occasions.

But as Paton's friend Bishop Trevor Huddleston has pointed out in *Naught for Your Comfort*, it is not the cut of the clothing that most characterized the gangs of *tsotsis* in Johannesburg's African townships in the 1950s:

Today in Alexandra and Sophiatown . . . it is not the clothes, it is the number, the gang, the weapons which are so terrifyingly evident. The *tsotsi* is youth rotting away and rotting with fear the society around him. He is problem number one in urban Africa.[2]

The terrifyingly cold-blooded gang that Paton created in another of his short stories, "The Waste Land," represents this rotting away to the point of ultimate inhumanity; but Spike, in "Death of a *Tsotsi*," has not reached such depths of degradation, but is a willing student at the reformatory. He attempts to break with his old gang and carries out his resolution to reform himself even in the face of threats from the gang members, who finally kill him rather than let him go free. Paton's theme in this story is an adaptation of the view that he had put forward so frequently in his writings on penal reform: that the real cure for crime is reform of society itself. Pending such general reform, successful restoration of individuals like Spike is almost impossible. The narrator says of Spike's death:

And this death would go on too, for nothing less than the reform of a society would bring it to an end. It was the menace of the socially frustrated, strangers to mercy, striking like adders for the dark reasons of ancient minds, at any who crossed their path. (*T.*, 106; *D.*, 69)

The story "Ha'penny"—a parable of a small boy's inborn need for social significance—offers a contrast to "Death of a *Tsotsi*." This story characterizes a homeless waif, who seems to the Principal to have invented an imaginary family for himself but who, in fact, has "adopted" a real family that does not want him. The Principal decides to break Ha'penny's fantasy rather than have him face rejection on his release from the reformatory. When the well-intentioned Principal reveals his knowledge of the facts to Ha'penny, "His whole brave assurance died within him, and he stood there exposed, not as a liar, but as a homeless child. . . . I had shattered the very foundations of his pride, and his sense of human significance" (*T.*, 55; *D.*, 31). The child falls ill and dies; and by his death, in a sense, passes judgment on the Principal, who had sensed "only the existence and not the measure of his desire" for human significance.

The remaining Diepkloof stories, "The Divided House" and "Spon-ono," present more complex characters who experience a struggle between the two sides of their natures. In *Towards the Mountain* Paton tells the story of Jacky, the boy torn between the pious desire to be a priest, and a life of theft, deception, and habitual use of *dagga* (i.e. marijuana). This boy provided both the model for Gertrude in *Cry, the Beloved Country* and the source of "The Divided House."

The fictional character Sponono in the story of that title is also based on an actual incorrigible who could not pass the final Diepkloof test of resisting temptation; yet who, by his charm and vanity, as well as his offences and repentances, staked out a special claim to the Principal's attention. The name Sponono, which in Zulu means a beautiful, shapely woman, is presumably a nickname accorded him by his gangmates. Paton has described Sponono, "the boy with the silver tongue," as one who could "care for the weak, rob the unsuspecting, forgive his enemies, rape a girl, all in the compass of a single month. Many years after he wrote to me from prison, 'I wish now that I had listened to you.'"[3]

In one incident in this story, Sponono threatens and robs a couple picnicking in a lonely area of Diepkloof farm. This is apparently the same incident that Paton referred to many years before in a lecture, "The Prevention of Crime," where, in making the point that people frequently invite crime through lack of foresight, he cited various incidents including this one: "A man wanders over to the Diepkloof farm and goes to sleep in the grass with fifty pounds in notes projecting invitingly from his pocket."[4]

The Diepkloof stories explore character and motivation, at times, perceptively; but they are not altogether self-contained. They have some of the qualities of fictional incidents that might be combined into a more sustained work such as a novel or a play. It may come as no surprise, therefore, to find three of them reworked into a play.

The Play *Sponono*

The longest of the Diepkloof stories, "Sponono," provides the core of the three-act play of the same title written by Paton in collaboration with Krishna Shah which, in 1964, became the first show from the workshop theater of the Union of African Artists with original actors and producer to be transferred directly to Broadway.[5] (A number of Athol Fugard's plays, and their African actors, subsequently moved directly to New York.)

The first two acts of *Sponono* combine the action of three of the Diepkloof stories: "Sponono," "Ha'penny," and "Death of a Tsotsi." They introduce also a chorus of African singers and drummers, and a clandestine "kangaroo" court presided over by Sponono which forces reformatory offenders to submit to the primitive test of plunging their arms into a pot of boiling water.

Except for the presence of the chorus on stage throughout, these first acts follow the mode of conventional realistic drama. They take thirteen scenes to bring together the stories of several characters from the short stories; in a sense, therefore, both acts are an exposition preparing the way for the extraordinary, expressionistic trial scene that constitutes Act Three, "The Court." (In this regard *Sponono* is reminiscent of Sean O'Casey's *The Silver Tassie*, in which the opening realistic scenes are followed by expressionistic scenes.) The first two acts of *Sponono* also have certain qualities that distinguish them sufficiently from their narrative sources in the short stories to mark the play *Sponono* as a wholly separate work. The play departs markedly from the sources first, in the greater development of some characters; and second, by the addition of the Chorus, which helps to provide a unifying framework for the whole, and to expand the significance of the action on stage.

In the play the character of the Principal assumes greater significance than in the Diepkloof stories, and his actions constitute a parable of that form of colonial rule in Southern Africa often described as Christian Trusteeship—a form advocated, for example, by Paton's mentor, Jan Hofmeyr. Furthermore, the Principal is presented as caught in the dilemma of any public man in a position of power who may not choose his mode of behavior as freely as a man of goodwill in private life. Other characters in the play are also more fully developed than their counterparts in the stories. For example, the opposing sides of Sponono's character are brought more sharply into contrast when he appears in different roles as "the first boy" and "the second boy," first welcoming and then robbing a pair of unsuspecting visitors. The girl Elizabeth is developed from a mere shadow in "Death of a Tsotsi" to an appealing character in the play. And Walter, the unregenerate *tsotsi*, brings to the stage an extraordinary measure of cold inhumanity.

Certain technical devices, no doubt introduced by Krishna Shah, also enhance the dramatic quality of the play, but these depend largely on imaginative production for their effectiveness. The first such device is employed in an imaginary Christmas scene, or charade, in which, for the benefit of the waif Ha'penny, the reformatory boys form a train and chug around in a circle with the accompaniment of chanting, stamping, and drumming, while the chorus sings. The second is a scene completely without dialogue in which a gang of *tsotsis* knife Spike Moletsane to death. Howard Taubman, reviewing the Broadway production of *Sponono*, found this to be a melodramatic scene "that would not be out of place in a B film."[6] But Gene Cole, commenting on a Chicago production, found this scene to be the point where "the play itself (as distinguished from the surrounding pagentry) becomes gripping and promises to take some sort of shape."[7]

The most dramatic device employed in *Sponono* is the Chorus of African drummers and singers. Without this Chorus, *Sponono* would be a drama focused on the problem of choosing freedom or repression as a reformatory instrument. With the Chorus, the dilemma becomes that of Africa herself; for a Chorus of drummers and singers, irrespective of what they drum or sing, is African in association. In fact, no dramatic device could be more symbolic of Africa. Since the traditional chants effectively establish an African atmosphere, the Chorus in *Sponono* is not merely peripheral to the action but contributes an essential element to the final effect of the play. Throughout the action the Chorus hovers on the stage's edge, making the spectators conscious of Africa waiting to pass judgment on the Principal.

The third act of *Sponono* turns to expressionism. Here, in a dream sequence, the Principal is brought to trial before Sponono and charged with having deserted not only his duty, but also the principles of his own religion—particularly the admonition to forgive seventy times seven times. In this trial scene, Sponono, although manacled, is enthroned as a mighty judge surrounded by councilors, warriors, drummers; all are in tribal costumes that suggest precolonial Africa as described by early explorers rather than the realities of Africa in the twentieth century. This scene, in which the boy passing judgment on the man symbolizes Africa judging her mentors, reaches an extraordinary pitch of dramatic intensity. Referring to this final scene, in which "all the strands are brought together and woven into a dramatic texture that has profound impact and meaning," Howard Taubman said of the Broadway production: "Here *Sponono* becomes fused, takes fire, and justifies its transplantation from South Africa with its South African ensemble."[8]

Beyond the implications of its African setting, *Sponono* deals with a fundamental human dilemma at several levels. There is the dilemma of Spike, the member of a juvenile gang who honestly attempts to reform, but finds himself "caught between two ways and both ways dangerous." Since this phrase is repeated like a refrain by Spike and Elizabeth, it takes on some of the implications of the dilemma of fear and faith that underlies *Cry, the Beloved Country*. There is also the dilemma of Sponono attracted to the good, and to the Principal whom he feels represents the good, yet unable to comprehend the Principal's distinction between "forgiveness" and "bearing the consequences of an act." And there is the further dilemma of the Principal who espouses a religion that teaches forgiveness "unto seventy times seven," yet who, in an office of public trust, must trim his sails to what is possible and practical.

Sponono was successfully played by racially mixed casts before integrated audiences in Durban and Johannesburg during 1962 and 1963, prior to the enactment of the ban on mixed theater audiences in South Africa. It was transferred with its South African cast and producer to the Court Theater, New York, in April 1964. Despite some favorable reviews stressing the play's significance—two of them by Howard Taubman in the *New York Times*—the play closed after a little more than two weeks at a time when another South African play, Athol Fugard's *Blood Knot*, was enjoying a successful New York run.

One reviewer, Richard A. Duprey, blamed *Sponono*'s tepid reception on the insensitivity of Broadway audiences:

> In the play *Sponono* which has sadly and unaccountably closed here in New York, we see the dilemma of forgiveness and punishment bared in stirring, absolutely electrifying, dramatic form. This play . . . was so right and so eloquent it provides another in a sequence of sad closings, in a cultural *milieu* that seems to prefer sensation and trash to real insight and emotional excitement.[9]

A successful production of *Sponono* at the small Parkway Theater at Hull House, Chicago, provides an interesting contrast to the play's lack of success in Broadway's commercial theater. This Hull House production, directed by Michael Miller, played to full houses throughout its scheduled run of ten weekends.[10] Richard Christiansen, reviewing the play for the *Chicago Daily News*, found *Sponono* to be "the damndest piece of theatre to be put on a Chicago stage this year."[11] He described it as "explosive, exciting, exuberant and smashingly singular in the kind of dramatic experience it offers." No doubt Michael Miller's imaginative production, and the professionalism of his drummers and dancers, contributed in good measure to this reviewer's enthusiastic response. But it is also worth noting that the Parkway Theater itself is a center for what Paton would call nonracial drama. In it, racially mixed casts play before integrated audiences who are, perhaps, more receptive to the work of Paton and Shah than Broadway audiences composed of conventional theater-goers.

Chapter Six

More Tragic Tales from a Troubled Land

The Public Themes

Besides the Diepkloof stories drawn from personal experience of reformatory life, Paton's short fiction includes a group of stories with public themes reflecting aspects of the implementation of *apartheid* and also the harsh suppression of opposition to it. These stories share the deeper vision and universal appeal of his early novels more closely than the Diepkloof stories do. They include four stories in *Tales from a Troubled Land* set outside the reformatory walls; and a much later addition, "Sunlight in Trebizond Street," the story of a prisoner held in solitary confinement while under interrogation by security police. Although this later story, like some of Kafka's, has no identifiable geographical setting, but has, rather, a symbolic location, a South African newspaper, fearing reprisal, was unwilling to publish it in 1969. (It later appeared in the collection *Knocking On the Door*.) With these stories of harsh, repressive action in a troubled land we might also classify Paton's short historical novel, *Ah, But Your Land Is Beautiful* (1981)—set against the background of Dr. Verwoerd's South Africa in the 1950s; and we may also consider in their political and social context the 1960 musical *Mkhumbane*, for which Paton provided the libretto, not because this musical had political themes, but because of the circumstances of its production during one of the worst weeks of violence and rioting in South Africa's history following the deaths of many Africans shot by police at Sharpeville on 21 March 1960.

Of the four stories in *Tales from a Troubled Land* set outside the reformatory walls, at least one, "The Waste Land," is a miniature masterpiece in the art of short fiction. Two others, which treat a South

African racial group not hitherto encountered in Paton's fiction, have qualities that resemble the best aspects of his novels. These two stories, "Life for a Life" and "Debbie Go Home," look as perceptively into the human condition of South Africa's Colored people (that is, the racial group composed of people of mixed blood) as *Cry, the Beloved Country* did into the plight of the Africans and *Too Late the Phalarope* into the agony of the Afrikaners.

A Kafkaesque World

"Debbie Go Home," the title story of the British edition, recounts a domestic conflict among the members of a Colored family. The father, Jim de Villiers, returns home early from his place of employment with the knowledge that the government's new Industrial Conciliation Act, popularly known as the Job Reservation Act, can turn him out of work by reserving solely for whites the occupation he has followed for years. His early return surprises his wife and teenage daughter as they are preparing a new gown for the girl to wear to the debutantes' ball for Colored girls—a racially segregated affair to be held at city hall in the presence of a high government official, the white Administrator of the Province.

Jim de Villiers angrily forbids the gown and the ball. His son Johnny, who belongs to a militant student organization at the university, supports him. Indeed, the son and other members of "the student Unity Movement" plan to picket the segregated debutantes' ball, and have already prepared signs and placards for the picket line bearing such slogans as "Welcome, spick little lickspittle" and "Debbie Go Home"—a local twist on "Yankee Go Home."

The force that sparks the domestic crisis in the de Villiers family arises from the mother's determination to obtain for her daughter at least "one night, in a nice dress and the coloured lights, dancing before the Administrator in the City Hall." We see her enlist the aid of her cynical, militant son to achieve her aim. But we become aware in the process of how the implementation of *apartheid* laws has shut against the younger generation doors to the attainment of a sense of personal worth that once seemed open to their elders.

In this respect "Debbie Go Home," together with its companion piece, "Life for a Life," has an important place in the canon of Paton's writings on South Africa—one equaled only by the two early novels. For if *Cry, the Beloved Country* embodies the most significant aspects of South Africa's social record in the 1940s and *Too Late the Phalarope* embodies the intense preoccupation with Pure Race that marked the opening of the 1950s, "Debbie Go Home" points to ominous signs of social realignment in the 1960s—a crucial shift in the traditional relationships among the races.

In "Debbie Go Home," Jim de Villiers returns from work with news of a new law: "It says the Minister can reserve any occupation. So we may have to go. We, we. The Coloured men." In his anger and frustration he curses the government and its representative, the provincial Administrator, for this and for the other legal cornerstones of *apartheid*, such as the law removing Colored voters from the common roll, the Group Areas Act that determines their place of residence, and the Population Registration Act that determines everyone's racial classification. As de Villiers puts it: ". . . a law that took away my job, and a law that took away my vote, and a law that's going to take away my house, all because I've a coloured skin" (*T.*, 83; *D.*, 16).

But in spite of Jim de Villiers's anger at the spate of *apartheid* legislation, his son Johnny accurately perceives a deeper cause for his father's frustration than the specific constraints of these laws. Johnny is aware of a bitter irony in his father's fulminations against the white Administrator; he knows how difficult it is for his father to be antiwhite, or even to conceive of being antiwhite. The older man had spent his formative years in an atmosphere that allowed him a measure of political freedom and independence. He had the right to vote, he was active in union affairs, and he supported General Smuts's United Party. He tells his son: "I was brought up in a world where we always hoped for the best . . . I was a Smuts man, don't forget." Johnny knows his father still retains the basic attitudes of his younger days when there was some point in striving after social and political advancement: "He hopes too much," says Johnny. "He knows what the world is like, yet he goes on hoping. And when the blow comes it knocks him down." In reply to his mother's query "Don't you hope?", Johnny gives the militant response: "I hope for nothing . . . nothing, nothing, nothing. I hope for nothing that I won't get my own way" (*T.*, 85; *D.*, 17).

If the split between generations manifested in "Debbie Go Home" truly reflected the feelings of most of the Cape Colored people in the 1960s, then it implies the approach of a new stage in South Africa's social evolution. The Cape Colored people, as a people of mixed blood, can belong neither to the camp of the white supremacists nor that of the black purists. As a minority group who could never hope to dominate the state, their inclination in the early part of the twentieth century had been to associate themselves with the ruling group. They have, in fact, always had much more in common with white South Africans than with indigenous Africans, for although they are descended in part from African as well as from European and Malayan forebears, they have no African cultural background.

Some years earlier, the South African novelist Sarah Gertrude Millin had written a story intended partly as a prophetic warning to South African white supremacists, in which a Colored person is represented as choosing to leave his group in an attempt to "pass for black" rather than "for white" as his relatives had traditionally done. The writer was suggesting that when Cape Colored people began to make such a choice deliberately, then real power in South Africa would have passed over from the whites to the nonwhites.

But Paton's "Debbie Go Home" looks more profoundly at the conflict between generations of Colored people than the story here referred to, which envisages the somewhat facile solution of the gradual swing of power. The social and political system to which Jim de Villiers's hopes of dignity and human significance were wedded had, indeed, crumbled. He was as he says, "a Smuts man"; and Smuts had always proclaimed, in his own quaint phrase, that the Cape Colored people were, "an appendage to the white race." But Paton does not set young Johnny's nihilistic program for the future against his father's lost cause; nor does he represent Johnny's militancy as more proper to the preservation of human dignity than his father's acceptance of the supporting role in which Smuts condescendingly cast the Cape Colored people.

The militant "Unity Movement" which Johnny supports is, no doubt, the fictional equivalent of the Non-European Unity Movement, a partly Trotskyite group that drew some support from Colored intellectuals in the Cape Province in the 1950s and 1960s. This group opposed the programs of the black African Nationalist Congress in the 1950s as strongly as it opposed the policies of the white Afrikaner Nationalist party. Its emergence at that time can be interpreted as one of a number of symptoms indicating that the trend of South African history may be toward a period of turmoil destined to belie all conventional expectations. Paton has remarked on this point: ". . . nor do I know otherwise how to interpret the emergence of the tragic and nihilistic movement known as the Non-European Unity Movement."[1]

Paton's story does not offer Johnny's nihilism, his cynicism, and his hopes for "nothing, nothing, nothing . . ." as a preferable alternative to his father's spiritlessness. Therefore, the lives of both father and son are equally tragic. "Debbie Go Home" offers no solution, unless it be the determination of Mrs. de Villiers to make the best of things—even to the extent of sending her daydreaming daughter to the debutantes' ball: "There's many a hard thing coming to her as well. I'd like her to have one night, in a nice dress, and the coloured lights, dancing before the Administrator in the city Hall. We get kicks aplenty. I wanted her to have a boost" (*T*., 83; *D*., 16). Mrs. de Villiers, even though she suffers much, is not a tragic figure in the sense that her husband and son are. Their state is determined by a powerful outside force against which they react in opposite, but equally futile, ways. She relies on an inner force—a love that expresses itself in giving, without any thought of self. When she says: "Go your own way. . . . But let me teach you one thing about giving. Don't keep half of it back," Johnny knows this is not the mere formula of words that his own proclaimed determination is: "I hope for nothing that I won't get my own way." Even he cannot resist the power of her inner force.

"Debbie Go Home" is a fine example of the storyteller's art, and it does not subordinate this art to some other purpose—whether such purpose be called social commentary or propaganda. The characters are recognizable human beings who are individual selves before they are South Africans or Cape Colored people or adherents of this or that political movement. Technically, "Debbie Go Home" which is developed primarily through dialogue, comes close to the art of drama, and could be staged effectively with but minor modification.

Death from Subcranial Bleeding

"Debbie Go Home" mirrors one aspect of the life of an urban Colored family within the legal framework of *apartheid*. Its companion story on the Cape Colored people, "Life for a Life," is set in a rural area where relations between the races are traditionally based on the more primitive philosophy of white supremacy called *Baasskap*. *Baasskap*, or Bossdom, is derived from an authoritarian attitude that recognizes only one permissible relationship between white and nonwhite, and that is a master-servant relationship resembling serfdom. An essential requirement of this relationship is that the servant should "know his place," and never aspire to equality on any ground.

In "Life for a Life," the central character, Enoch Maarman, a Colored man of Hottentot descent, is head shepherd on the estate of Kroon. He is described as "a man who had never hurt another in his long gentle life, a man who like the great Christ was a lover of sheep and of little children." But by sending his son to the university, Enoch transgressed the fundamental law of *Baasskap* that required Colored shepherds to "teach their children to know forever their station." The master of Kroon farm, Big Baas Flip, therefore ordered that the shepherd's son should never again be permitted to set foot on his land, not even to visit his parents. (It was no doubt some spiritual kin to Baas Flip who celebrated the Nationalist party election victory in 1948 by burning rural schools for black children). When, some time later, Big Baas Flip was found murdered, apparently by thieves who took away a heavy safe, the local police focused their investigation on the head shepherd who had brought suspicion on himself by failing to "know his place."

"Life for a Life" has two complementary subthemes. One is embodied in a sadistic detective, Robbertse, who derives great pleasure from inflicting pain: "he hated to see any colored man holding up his head, he hated to see any colored man anywhere but on his knees or his stomach." Robbertse is more than a sadist; he has a touch of madness, real or feigned—an unreasoning hate that might be described as racial paranoia. Robbertse is not a type of the Afrikaner police officer, for when fellow officers are present they restrain him when he goes too far. He is a type of the extreme racist anywhere, who exhibits the apparently motiveless malignity with which deeply rooted race hatred is sometimes expressed. To such a mind, persons of another race are inherently evil—as Jews were to Hitler, or as Othello may have been to Iago. And such a mind will, like Iago, take suspicion for surety. At nightfall, "which was no time to be looking for a safe," Robbertse came to carry out an earlier warning that Enoch would have to show him the place "where your friends hid the safe." Enoch does not return home from this expedition, and it is given out that he slipped in the river bed and crushed his head on a stone.

The second subtheme is inherent in the efforts of Enoch's wife, Sara, to discover the exact cause of her husband's death and to recover his body, which has already been hurriedly buried. In the prevailing circumstances, Sara, like a character in a Kafka novel, is confronted by a vague power, malignant and irrational, that makes every rational step absurd. There are official answers to everything, but none of them fit.

Like Kafka's stories, "Life for a Life" is parable literature. It is a parable of *Baasskap* which, with men like Robbertse as its instrument, may condone brutality that "teaches a lesson." Brutality condoned involves others through complicity; so Enoch's death certificate states simply, *"death due to sub-cranial bleeding."* Police officers who might not themselves have harmed Enoch, accept without investigation the story that he slipped and fell, and they arrange hurried burial for the body on "an order from a high person." Paton's own summing up of one of Kafka's novels seems applicable here: "Kafka's story *The Trial* gives a frightening picture of the insignificance of man when he is confronted with the power of a cruel State. A man believing himself to be innocent is visited by the security police, taken to the court, tried by a judge who thunders at him, all this in such an atmosphere of fantasy and inexplicability that one realizes that one needs much more than innocence to save one from malignant authority."[2]

Looking back from the perspective of the 1980s, Paton's "Life for a Life" appears tragically prophetic of the disturbing series of "accidental" deaths of black opponents of *apartheid* while in the custody of South African security police. One of the first to die under mysterious circumstances in detention was Looksmart Ngudle, in September

1963. Another was the Moslem Imam Haron, commemorated in Paton's poem "Death of a Priest" in *Knocking at the Door*, who, in 1969, "fell down the stairs" while being interrogated by police. A more widely known instance was that of the black consciousness leader Steve Biko, whose death while under interrogation in 1977 was attributed to "head injuries." In an editorial on Steve Biko's death, *Reality*, November 1977, said, ". . . during the last few years deaths in detention have become commonplace. Indeed one could go further, and say that, during the past eighteen months there has been . . . an average of more than one a month."

There is a suggestion of another dimension of parable in "Life for a Life." This arises from the explicit comparison of the head shepherd, Enoch Maarman, to the Good Shepherd, Christ: "a man who like the great Christ was a lover of sheep and of little children. . . ." This comparison, made in the mind of Enoch's wife, Sara, could be merely a conventional analogy. But there is also a suggestion that Enoch is an innocent victim demanded by the preservers of *Baasskap*, as the Chief Priests demanded Christ as a victim: "it is expedient that one man should die for the people." Or to express it as Paton did in his remarks on Kafka: "one needs more than innocence to save one from malignant authority." The Maarmans knew that with Big Baas Flip murdered: "Someone must pay for so terrible a crime, and if not the one who did it, then who better than the one who could not grieve" (*T.*, 10; *D.*, 46).

Even with this additional element of parable, it seems unlikely that Paton intends Enoch Maarman to represent Christ directly. He records that he once attempted, and rejected, a novel "about Christ's return to South Africa in the form of a young Afrikaner"; he is, therefore, aware of the difficulties of this form of fiction. If one examines "Life for a Life" in the light of the careful analysis of the literary problems of presenting Christ in novels or plays, on which Paton and Liston Pope collaborated in "The Novelist and Christ," it seems clear that the parallels between Enoch and Christ are limited to the indirection of parable, and that they do not constitute an attempt to present a symbolic figure representing Christ.[3]

The same may be said of Paton's poem "Death of a Priest," where the Imam is represented, symbolically, as sharing Christ's sufferings:

Most honourable do not bestir yourself,
The man is dead.
He fell down the stairs and died.
And all his wounds can be explained
Except the holes in his hands and feet
And the long deep thrust in his side. (*KD*, 227)

One, in particular, of the nonreformatory stories in *Tales from a Troubled Land* is less reminiscent of Kafka than of the horrors of Dostoevski or Dante's *Inferno*. This very short story, "The Wasteland," is a masterpiece of artistic economy. In it, as in *Cry, the Beloved Country*, we encounter a society in which a code of conduct has been destroyed and not replaced by a better one. In this case, the subsociety of the urban juvenile gang provides the ultimate instance of cold-blooded dehumanization, for loyalty to the gang is demanded even above natural filial loyalty. The central character, like several other Paton characters, is a good man, hardworking and law-abiding, who falls victim to criminal attack. Returning home with his wages, he is waylaid in the dark by a gang that includes his son. The situation has the seeds of melodrama; but the story is told in such a cold shorthand of indirection and understatement that the reader is left to envision the ultimate horror of the encounter for himself. Again, as in *Too Late the Phalarope*, fear, foreboding, and terror are expertly evoked, as is the cold-blooded inhumanity of the gang members. Just when they have come to believe that their victim and his money have eluded them, one of them stumbles over a dead body and calls out, in fine irony, "We are saved . . . here is the man." But the corpse is one of their own members, killed when their intended victim struck out blindly in his terror. And the hunted man hears again the name of his son as the gang members callously toss the body under the abandoned truck where their quarry is hiding.

The final nonreformatory story in *Tales from a Troubled Land* is more farcical than tragic and provides a good contrast to "Life for a Life." This story, "A Drink in the Passage," is Paton's lightest variation on one of his favorite themes: that of people of different races trying awkwardly, yet honestly, to reach out across barriers and touch each other as persons. Paton introduces us to an African journalist and sculptor, who relates his own story of how a young Afrikaner who admired his work invited him to his home for a drink. There is awkward, fumbling goodwill on both sides, with the young white man completely unaware that in his attempt at comradeship within the bounds of white traditional customs he is deeply embarrassing the African.

Lewis Nkosi, an African journalist formerly on the staff of the Johannesburg magazine *Drum*, says in his *Home and Exile* that Paton's story is a report of an actual incident in the life of one of the black journalists associated with *Drum*.[4] The story, though slight, is well done; and it provides another instance of Paton's liking for recasting actual events in fictional form for the sake of the light they shed on the human dilemma in South Africa.

Sharpeville and the Premiere of Mkhumbane

Apartheid laws upholding total racial separation not only forbid racially mixed marriages, schools, and places of habitation, but for a time, at least, they also forbade mixed theater audiences and racially mixed casts. It was in the context of such restrictions, as well as his determination to be "militantly non-racial" that Paton once declared: "I, myself, do not wish any play of mine to be presented before segregated audiences. . . . Better no theatre at all than a colour-bar theatre."[5] With Athol Fugard and others, and particularly the primarily black Union of African Artists, Paton contributed to an attempt to bring into being in South Africa a nonracial drama countenancing racially mixed casts and integrated audiences.

In 1960 he provided the libretto for the musical *Mkhumbane*, with music by the black composer Todd Matshikiza. The work was specially written for the South African Institute of Race Relations, partly with the object of giving African actors and actresses a chance to display their gifts. *Mkhumbane* was first presented in the Durban city hall during the last week of March 1960; a week that, by coincidence, was to be the week of greatest tension in recent South African history.

On Monday, 21 March 1960, police fired on crowds of demonstrators at Sharpeville in the Transvaal and Langa in the Cape Province. At Sharpeville, an African township adjacent to Vereeniging where the Boer War armistice had been signed, sixty-nine Africans were killed by this police action, and one hundred and eighty wounded. This tragedy initiated a period of intense fear and strife in South Africa. Ex-Chief Albert Luthuli, leader of the African National Congress, ceremoniously burned his Pass Book and called on all Africans to observe a day of mourning on 28 March by staying away from work. On that same day Parliament introduced an Unlawful Organizations Bill empowering the government to ban the two African political organizations, the African National Congress and the Pan-African Congress. On 30 March, the government proclaimed a national State of Emergency; and, in the early morning of that day, the police detained 234 men and women of all races, including ex-Chief Luthuli and also Peter Brown, the national chairman of Paton's Liberal party.

Against this background, with thousands of Africans marching through the streets of Durban and Capetown, and with the white population of South Africa in a state of fear and anxiety, *Mkhumbane* was presented to mixed audiences in Durban. Paton recalls that "during this momentous week, we played to full houses, people of all kinds and races, in Durban City Hall. It was indeed a moving experience to go into that hall and see there the absence of all fear and hate."[6] This first production of *Mkhumbane* was successful; but efforts to revive it in South Africa have not been successful because the late Todd Matshikiza's score, on which the musical depends more than it does on Paton's libretto, has been unavailable.

Besides the historic occasion of its first production, and its appeal to racially mixed audiences in South Africa, *Mkhumbane* has significance as an instance of the extraordinary vitality of the theater among Africans in South African cities during the 1950s and early 1960s. To say that *Mkhumbane* was written to give African actors and actresses a chance to display their gifts means precisely that these actors were, in fact, gifted and that what they lacked was not talent, but suitable plays to perform. (Paton had earlier written a play, *Last Journey*, about David Livingstone, for the Waddington Players of Lusaka, Zambia. It was performed and reviewed—and described in the first edition of this study—but he does not intend to publish it.)[7]

Chapter Seven

The Liberal Party:
Hope for South Africa and *The Long View*

Moral Geography: Stony Soil; Stern Virtues

In his autobiography, *Towards the Mountain* (1980), Paton characterized his Scottish-born father, James Paton, as a strict authoritarian
who sometimes ruled his family harshly. In the light of this autobiography it seems clear that some personal experience of a father-son
conflict lent touches of color to the portrait of Jakob van Vlaanderen,
the authoritarian father in *Too Late the Phalarope*. But these real and
fictional fathers differ in essentials. James Paton exercised no power
outside his family circle, and was a diffident man in public. Jakob van
Vlaanderen, on the other hand, was an influential man of great power
in national politics who ruled both his immediate family and a wide
circle of the Afrikaner community like an Old Testament patriarch.
Jakob is more than an interesting psychological type. He is an
allegorical figure personifying attitudes shaped by Afrikaner racial
experience.

The primordial Afrikaners—the late seventeenth- and early eigh-
teenth-century "trek-Boers"—first established themselves inland from
the Cape of Good Hope in the inhospitable, semidesert soil of the
Karoo area. For almost a century these trek-Boers lived an isolated
frontier life in the harsh environment of the Karoo, cut off, meanwhile, from the social thought then evolving in Europe concerning
equality and the rights of man—ideas that led elsewhere to the
American and French revolutions. Generations of these unschooled
and isolated cattle farmers, for whom European ideas ceased to count,
developed their own social norms in a hostile African environment.

In *Hope for South Africa* (1958), his brief history of South African liberalism, Paton discusses some of the permanent effects of the harsh Karoo experience of the trek-Boers on the character and outlook of their descendants. "No visitor to South Africa should fail to see the Karoo," says Paton, "if he wishes to understand an important chapter in the genesis of the Afrikaner people." And he says of the Karoo: "It is a hard country, encouraging what are sometimes called the masculine qualities of courage, tenacity, inflexibility"; and, conversely, "discouraging the feminine qualities of gentleness, kindness, and compassion" (14).

Approval of the masculine virtues is commonly expressed in South Africa by the use of the Afrikaans term *kragdadigheid*—a word that means effectiveness, or "strength in action," but which has come to mean in the political arena, "rule by show of force." In a newspaper article addressing the Nationalist party leaders in May 1973 on the twenty-fifth anniversary of their coming to power, Paton said; "You admire power, determination, physical courage, *kragdadigheid*. Moral courage in other people you are suspicious of. You throw out your Malherbes, Marquards, Kriges, Beyers Naudés. You shy away from love, compassion, and mercy, even from the words. You suspect those who use them of being Communist tools."[1] In short, Paton ascribes to these latter day Afrikaner leaders an outlook like that of the patriarch, Jakob, in *Too Late the Phalarope* who was enraged by the feminine qualities in his son Pieter, even though the boy manifested unmistakable masculine qualities also.

Continuing in *Hope for South Africa* to interpret the effects of Karoo life on the genesis of the Afrikaner people, Paton says that while conditions of isolation and wilderness have commonly led to degeneration, this was rarely the case in the Karoo because of the trekkers' veneration for the Bible, and their sense of identification with the chosen people of the Old Testament. The trekkers were attracted, in particular, says Paton, by the stories of the patriarchs; for these seemed most relevant to their hard and lonely life: "And who could have been nearer to the patriarchs than they themselves, as they moved in the wilderness with their flocks and herds, with their menservants and their maidservants, among wild men and wild beasts with no protection but their rifles and their God?" (15). It is not surprising, he says, that, in these conditions of frontier life, the Old Testament seemed more relevant than the New, and that "the God of Israel was more comprehensible than the Lover of mankind."

Jakob van Vlaanderen was such a latter-day patriarch. Even in the mid-twentieth century, in the aftermath of World War II, he could countenance no falling off from the strict code that had sustained his forebears who had preserved their church, language, and racial identity in the alien surroundings of the Karoo. Jakob is a fictional figure; but he is an authentic reflection of the patriarchial spirit still flourishing among leaders of Afrikanerdom. These leaders rule by *kragdadigheid*. They fear liberal attitudes regarding race. And they enforce the iron laws against racial mixing. Concerned—perhaps even obsessed—with preserving their national integrity, Afrikaner leaders have traditionally tended to rely on constraint and denial of freedoms to preserve their vision of the "good" society. Consequently, in the political sphere, they are suspicious of, and hostile toward, those who value individual freedoms more highly than the preservation of Afrikaner racial identity such as the four Afrikaner intellectuals named above (and in the notes to this chapter): Malherbe, Marquard, Krige, and Beyers Naudé.

Proponents of human rights and freedoms seeking equal opportunities for all races have rarely been welcome in Afrikaner-ruled South Africa. They are commonly spoken of as liberalists—a term implying attachment to a wrong-headed philosophy, disregard for moral restraint, and the condoning of sexual promiscuity particularly across racial lines. Furthermore, many Afrikaner Nationalists thought that *liberalists* were blind to the dangers of communism. In 1946 Paton's friend Jan Hofmeyr had warned, as deputy prime minister, against "the growing tendency to describe as Communist . . . any who asked for fair play for all races or who suggested that non-Europeans really should be treated as the equal of Europeans before the law" (*SAT*, 326; *H*,422). But the Nationalist party, on gaining power, made the terms of their Suppression of Communism Act (1950) sufficiently broad to apply to anyone who opposed *apartheid* and advocated social change including anti-Communist Liberals many of whom were banned under its provisions in the 1960s.[2] Mr. J. B. Vorster, the minister for justice at that period and later prime minister, took seriously his own maxim: "Communism kills, but Liberalism leads you into an ambush to be killed."

A Liberal Tradition

There was no formally constituted Liberal party at the national level in the Union of South Africa before 1953; but there was a lively liberal tradition deriving elements from a variety of sources, one of which was the early nineteenth-century reform movement in Britain. This British movement had success in the reform of Parliament, lowering the property qualification for voting rights, and the abolition by acts of the British Parliament, first, of the slave trade in 1832, and then of the institution of slavery in 1834. British law was then in force at the Cape of Good Hope which Britain had occupied during the Napoleonic Wars—temporarily in 1795 and permanently in 1806—and the abolition Acts were immediately enforced.

The slave-owning Boer farmers resented the freeing of their slaves by an occupying power. They resented also, perhaps with some reason, the inadequate arrangements for compensation which was payable only in London. But most of all they resented being placed on an equal footing before the law with their former slaves. Refusing to live on such terms of equality, some trekked inland under leaders like Piet Retief, giving as one of their reasons—in the words of Retief's sister, Anna Steenkamp:

. . . the shameful and unjust proceedings with reference to the freeing of our slaves; and yet it is not so much their freeing which drove us to such lengths, as their being placed on an equal footing with Christians, contrary to the laws of God, and the natural distinctions of race and colour, so that it was intolerable for any decent Christian to bow down beneath such a yoke; wherefore we withdrew in order to preserve our doctrines in purity.[3]

These *voortrekkers*, as they were called, founded the Boer republics of the Orange Free State and the Transvaal so that they might be beyond the reach of British law. The constitution of the Transvaal declared that in matters of race there should be "no equality in church or state."

While the Boers ruled themselves in their independent republics, a measure of representative self-government was introduced into the British-ruled Cape Colony from which they had migrated. Under the terms of a constitution granted by Britain, an elected Parliament was established and voting rights were extended, as in Britain, on the basis of property qualification, not on the basis of race. Although the number of African and mixed-race voters was not great, the principle of voter registration survived in the Cape Province until the time of Union in 1910 when, in the aftermath of the Boer War, the four separate political units in South Africa—Cape Province, Natal, Orange Free State, and Transvaal—were brought together into the Union of South Africa. At that time the Cape Liberals, English-speaking and Afrikaans-speaking alike, sought to extend the Cape's common-roll franchise to the whole Union. The three other provinces rejected this extension, but agreed that the Cape should retain its common-roll franchise, and the Union constitution guaranteed that no change could be made affecting the common roll without a two-thirds majority of both houses of parliament voting together.

In 1936 the Hertzog-Smuts coalition government collected the necessary two-thirds majority—with only Jan Hofmeyr and ten others voting in opposition—and removed African voters from the Cape common roll, but permitted them to elect "Natives' representatives" in separate elections. Cape Colored (mixed-race) voters were not affected. After the Nationalist party election victory in 1948, the prime minister, Dr. Malan, sought to remove the Cape Colored voters from the common roll to a separate roll which would have permitted them to elect "Coloured Representatives" to Parliament. This initiated a constitutional struggle in the course of which the Liberal party was formed.

At first the strongest opposition to Dr. Malan's constitutional change came from Jan Smuts's United party and a World War II veterans organization called the Torch Commando. The Torch Commando movement, with its enthusiastic rallies, was the crest of the wave of traditional white liberalism in South Africa, and it broke on the traditional rock: although united in support of the rights of nonwhites, the white Torch Commando movement divided on the issue of collaboration with Coloured movements seeking the same goal. Its members were not prepared to make common cause with nonwhites in an interracial—or nonracial—movement. But the Liberal party which emerged in 1953 was prepared to accept a common cause and common membership. This willingness to make common cause on a nonracial basis was so distinctive a mark of the spirit of the new Liberal party that Chief Albert Luthuli traced the party's origin to the Defiance Campaign of 1952 when Patrick Duncan (son of a former governor general of South Africa) and Manilal Gandhi (son of Mahatma Gandhi) led groups of white and Indian volunteers to join Africans defying *apartheid* laws. [4] (The Defiance Campaign opens the action of Paton's third novel *Ah, But Your Land Is Beautiful* and Patrick Duncan, Chief Luthuli, and Manilal Gandhi appear as characters in it.)

The decision to found a Liberal party was taken at a meeting of the South African Liberal Association in Cape Town on 9 May 1953. Margaret Ballinger, MP, was elected president, with Leo Marquard and Alan Paton as vice-presidents. Dr. Oscar Wolheim was elected national chairman, with Leslie Rubin as national vice-chairman. At first the party favored limited franchise for Africans and other nonwhites based on a gradual extension of the old Cape franchise. But in time it adopted a policy of universal voting rights in accord with the popular African motto, "One man, one vote." To begin with, Liberal party membership was predominantly white, but within ten years it was predominantly African.

Paton in the Liberal Party

In 1952 Paton postponed work on his biography of Jan Hofmeyr while Mrs. Hofmeyr lived. He was for a time uncertain of his future course. Feeling at a crossroads, and troubled by the spate of new laws and regulations designed to perpetuate *apartheid*, he decided to devote a year or more to working in a tuberculosis settlement for Africans at Botha's Hill, Natal. Botha's Hill was then a new project with only two buildings on a thirty-acre site. While there, Paton intended to work with his hands, as he had frequently done at Diepkloof, to help build sufficient accommodations for 600 people. In response to an inquiry from the *Saturday Review*, he wrote in August 1953: "At the moment my wife and I are at the Toc-H TB Settlement at Botha's Hill. The task of the settlement is to help Africans who have had TB to return to normal life. We have given ourselves to this work for a year and are enjoying it." He goes on to say, "We are also working for the new Liberal Party, whose aim is to accustom South Africa to the idea that our only hope is to open the doors of our society to all people who are ready for it, no matter what their race or colour."[5]

While at Botha's Hill, Paton wrote *South Africa and Her People*, a volume in the Portraits of the Nations series designed for high-school students in Britain and America. In the United States it was published under the title *The Land and People of South Africa*. Paton presents South Africa to his young readers in the guise of a conducted tour. He avoids controversial issues during the course of the "tour," and saves his estimate of the current situation in South Africa for a closing chapter that looks toward the future.

As books of this kind indicate, Paton continued to live as a professional writer during the early years of the Liberal party. His duties to the party were not onerous since the organizational tasks fell primarily to the chairman, Oscar Wolheim, and the vice-chairman, Leslie Rubin. He undertook an extensive tour of the United States in 1954, at the invitation of *Collier's*, to report on race relations in America; and he set down his views in two articles: "The Negro in America Today," and "The Negro in the North." [6] During this tour he also addressed the World Council of Churches meeting at Evanston, Illinois, and visited Yale University to receive the honorary degree of Doctor of Humane Letters.

Paton returned to the United States in 1956 while Robert Yale Libott's dramatized version of *Too Late the Phalarope* was being prepared for the Broadway stage. This play opened its Broadway run at the Belasco Theater on 11 October 1956, with Barry Sullivan as Pieter van Vlaaderen and the Scottish actor Finlay Currie as Jakob. Reviews of the play are surprisingly similar to some of the reviews of *Sponono* eight years later—lamenting the lack of public interest in drama with a serious theme. John Gassner remarks in his *Theatre at the Crossroads* that "the work earned respect for everyone associated with it. But *Too Late the Phalarope* could not win its bout with the Broadway public."[7]

It was during his 1956 visit to New York, when literary matters seemed once more about to occupy his interest that Paton received news of his election as national chairman of the Liberal party. Averse as he was to public political life, he accepted the election as a call to duty and purposefully undertook the task of organizing the Liberal party. He also continued to write, but now much of what he wrote was directly concerned with the policies and aims of the Liberal party—as is the case with such books and pamphlets as *Hope for South Africa*, *The People Wept*, and *The Charlestown Story*. But one of the tasks that he undertook in 1956 that was to remain with him as a source of concern for ten years, was an unexpected one arising from the dramatic South African Treason Trial that began in December 1956 and continued for four years.

On 5 December 1956, 156 South Africans of all races were arrested and charged with treason under the Suppression of Communism Act. Those arrested included such African leaders as Chief Albert Luthuli, subsequently a recipient of the Nobel Peace Prize, and Professor Z. K. Matthews, a highly respected educator. On the day after these arrests, Paton, together with Bishop Reeves of Johannesburg, Dr. Ellen Hellman of the Institute of Race Relations, Alex Hepple, a Labor party member of Parliament, and Judge Frank Lucas, organized the Treason Trial Defence Fund to enable those accused of treason to have adequate defense.

No one could then foresee how long and how costly the Treason Trial was to be. During the four years that the trial lasted, the Defence Fund collected several hundred thousand dollars for legal expenses, and also to provide some aid for the dependents of those detained. When the verdict was finally given on 29 March 1961, all the accused were acquitted. But the organizers of the Defence Fund were not able to close the books on their undertaking because, in the meantime, there arose the need to help with the defence of a new and growing group of prisoners.

As a consequence of the State of Emergency declared in South Africa in 1960 following the shootings at Sharpeville, many people were arrested and detained under the administration's emergency powers. To draw attention to the numbers imprisoned, Paton with Mrs. Albert Luthuli, Fatima Meer, and Manilal Gandhi's widow led night-long fasting and prayers—in which they were joined by hundreds of Africans and Indians on 31 May 1960, the day on which fifty years of Union was being celebrated in South Africa.[8] To assist those in prison, the fund organized for the Treason Trial was broadened in purpose in 1960, and renamed the Defence and Aid Fund.

Defence and Aid was soon attacked as a subversive organization, and those associated with it were denounced by some newspapers as "Catspaws of the Communists" and as "fellow-travelers." During 1965, opposition to the fund intensified, particularly when the government of Holland donated $28,000 to it. In answering critics of Defence and Aid, Paton pointed out that even those presumed guilty had the right to adequate legal representation, and that unless this right was conceded, the administration of justice itself was in danger of erosion: "It is to me a duty owing not only to the accused person, not only to the judge, but supremely to our society, that adequate defence should be secured in a society where passions are so intense, and where many white South Africans regard security as far more important than justice."[9] But Defence and Aid was, nevertheless, banned under the terms of the all-purpose Suppression of Communism Act. The ban was announced at midnight on 20 March 1966. Early next morning the security police raided regional offices and the homes of some committee members. They visited Paton's home that morning, too, and took away papers related to the fund. He gives a vivid account of this incident in *For You Departed*.

Contact and *The Long View*

In February 1958 supporters of the Liberal party's view launched a new journal of opinion called *Contact*. Paton was one of the Board of Directors of this journal and wrote a regular column for it during its first year of publication under the heading "The Long View." His "Long View" essay for the first issue of *Contact* was written from Nigeria where he had gone as a delegate of the Anglican Church to the first All-African Church Conference at Ibadan, in January 1958. It told of Nigerian anger at the policies of *apartheid*, and asserted the Liberal party's support for a nonracial democracy in South Africa. Paton wrote twenty-three "Long View" essays for *Contact* during its first year of publication on various aspects of *apartheid*, particularly the complex Group Areas Act designed not only to separate African, Indian, and white living areas, but ultimately to restrict Africans to citizenship in designated tribal areas called "Homelands." He closed the series in January 1959 with the essay "The Days of White Supremacy Are Over." In the course of it he repeated the parable of a man knocking on a barred closed door that he used on several occasions, and that supplies the title of the collection of his shorter writings edited in 1975 by Colin Gardner:

> A white South African is a man who hears about Leopoldville (the Congo) today and forgets it tomorrow. Nevertheless this last column is for him, he being my brother in blood.
> I went to my brother and said, "Brother, a man is knocking at the door."
> My brother said, "Is he a friend or enemy?"
> "I have asked him," I said, "but he replies that you will not and can not know until you have opened the door."
> The days of white supremacy are over. Every politician, whatever his creed, should keep that in mind. Any political theory based on some other assumption is a waste of time. (*LV.*, 135)

Paton wrote three separate series of essays for *Contact*'s column "The Long View." These were subsequently collected and edited with related material by Edward Callan in *The Long View* (1968). After Paton completed his first series from February 1958 to February 1959, Peter Brown, who succeeded him as chairman of the Liberal party, wrote the "Long View" column until his imprisonment on 30 March 1960. After Brown's imprisonment, Paton wrote his second series of "Long View" essays until 31 August 1960, when the state of emergency ended and Brown once more replaced him. Just over three years later, when banning orders were served on Brown, the "Long View" column was taken up again by Paton in January 1964. Paton persevered with his third "Long View" series through all *Contact*'s vissicitudes—including the banning of four editors—until October 1966 when the magazine virtually ceased to exist. Its story parallels that of the Liberal party.

Contact began in February 1958 as a well-designed magazine comparable in appearance to any journal produced by a competent professional staff. At first it appeared every two weeks, and had well-printed, illustrated, 14½-by-11-inch pages. For the first year or two it attracted a substantial amount of advertising, including that of major national business concerns such as oil and tobacco companies. But the copies of *Contact* from 1960 to 1963 no longer proclaim it to be a successfully produced news magazine. They vary abruptly in size, and noticeably lack advertising—particularly that of national business concerns. There are fewer issues on the shelves, too, for *Contact* had changed from a brave fortnightly magazine to monthly newspaper "For United Non-Racial Action." The issue for August 1964 is mimeographed, with this explanation of a "temporary change" by the editors:

Since 1960 this newspaper has endured most of the penalties heaped on those who speak out openly and in clear opposition in a police state. It has suffered the disruption of police searches and of several prosecutions; it has had two editors and other members of its staff banned; its selling agents have been repeatedly harassed; and three or four times it has had to change its printers. The last change was made, unfortunately, with very little notice and came too late for suitable alternative printing arrangements to bring the newspaper out before the end of August.

To this the editors add the brave assertion:

. . . we shall continue to publish as long as we have one person with one typewriter and one machine left to print or duplicate what we believe must be said from inside South Africa.[10]

Contact continued to keep up its registration as a newspaper and to appear monthly in a variety of printed forms. By July 1965, five editors and six staff members and contributors had been served banning orders. More than thirty-five printers, fearing the consequences to themselves, had refused to print the paper, and the staff was forced to do the job. By late 1965, *Contact* was reduced to a few folded mimeographed sheets, and it finally gave up its registration as a newspaper. In 1966, it no longer appeared in monthly issues, but only from time to time. All other radical newspapers in South Africa had by this time "collapsed of their own accord"; even the highly reputable *Forum*, the journal of liberal opinion founded in 1938 to promote Jan Hofmeyr's philosophy, had ceased publication for lack of support. *Contact*, nevertheless, kept its promise to continue publishing "as long as we have one person with one typewriter and one machine left to print or duplicate what we believe must be said."

By 1966 *Contact* had, in fact, little more than one typewriter in its office. The office had been raided at times not only by the police, but also by thugs who removed or destroyed equipment; even the office telephone was given up to avoid the frequent interruption of threatening telephone calls. A final issue, without the "Long View" column, appeared in 1967, the year the Liberal party was dissolved because of a law that made it illegal "for a white person and a black person to belong to the same political party" (*FYD*, 132).

The significance of this sketch of the history of *Contact* in an account of the writings of Alan Paton is this: not once, even during *Contact*'s worst trials, did Paton fail to produce his regular column. From the second half of 1965 onward, each issue of *Contact* consisted mainly of Paton's column, together with brief accounts of judicial bannings culled from other newspapers. Paton's regular contributions demonstrate his determination to stand behind *Contact*'s nonracial program. But from the literary viewpoint, his contributions to *Contact* also constitute a substantial portion of the creative work of a writer who has thought deeply about the dangers of racism—not only for South Africa but for the world at large in the twentieth century. The same may be said of writings in *Reality: A Journal of Liberal Opinion*, founded by Paton and other Natal liberals in 1969, for which he regularly provides editorials and articles.

1960: State of Emergency and Freedom Award

In 1959 Paton gave up the chairmanship of the Liberal party to return to work on his biography of Jan Hofmeyr. He was given the specially created post of President of the Liberal Party and he was succeeded as chairman by Peter Brown, who took over his active duties, including the "Long View" column for *Contact*. But his work on the biography was interrupted by the State of Emergency declared in South Africa following the events at Sharpeville in March 1960. In the early morning of 30 March 1960, the police detained 234 men and women of all races, among them Peter Brown. Brown was kept in prison without trial for four months, and Paton once again undertook the active duties of chairman of the Liberal party: "At real personal risk and cost, he ran the national office of the Party and led the Party in all ways."[11]

Paton wrote his second series of essays for "The Long View" in *Contact* while replacing Peter Brown during this emergency period. His task was now doubly difficult: not only were the tensions within South Africa extreme, but some supporters of the Liberal party's nonracial policies were discouraged by the violence in the Congo. They were discouraged, in particular, by the racist aspects of this violence, and by Mr. Lumumba's demands that *white* United Nations troops be withdrawn. Paton did not evade these sensitive subjects in his new series, but addressed himself to them courageously.

In the midst of the tensions and pressures of the State of Emergency, supporters of the Liberal party were heartened by Paton's nomination for the 1960 Freedom Award. The Freedom Award has been conferred annually since 1943 by Freedom House, New York, on outstanding defenders of civil liberties and the ideals of democracy. Freedom House, New York—headquarters of several associated organizations—was so named to symbolize opposition to what Hitler's Braunhaus in Munich stood for; since World War II Freedom House has worked to oppose totalitarian systems of both the Fascist and Communist varieties, and to further justice and individual freedoms. Earlier recipients of the annual Freedom Award include Sir Winston Churchill, Franklin Roosevelt, Dwight Eisenhower, George C. Marshall, and Dag Hammarskjold.

In preparing to nominate the recipient of its annual Award, Freedom House first defines the dominating issue currently affecting freedom, and then decides who best symbolizes the struggle in that area. In the late 1950s its members emphasized the issue of race relations in the United States; in 1960 they defined worldwide racism to be the prevailing issue: "And among the fighters for freedom one name stood out—a citizen of South Africa, a brilliant novelist with a tender heart and tough mind . . . Alan Paton was the logical choice for the Freedom Award of 1960."[12]

Paton came to New York to receive the award at the annual Freedom House ceremony honoring recipients on 5 October 1960. His presence aroused great interest, and "representatives of the literary and political worlds came in such numbers that many had to be turned away." President Eisenhower sent a message of congratulations which read, in part, "Through his brave and sensitive writings on behalf of the underprivileged, Mr. Paton has worked to remove the social and racial barriers which plague mankind. In striving to achieve for all men recognition of the dignity to which they are entitled, he stands as a fine symbol of Freedom House."

Archibald MacLeish, who presented the award, characterized Paton as follows:

To live at the center of the contemporary maelstrom; to see it for what it is and to challenge the passions of those who struggle in it beside him with the voice of reason—with, if he will forgive me, the enduring reasons of love; to offer the quiet sanity of the heart in a city yammering with the crazy slogans of fear; to do all this at the cost of tranquillity and the risk of harm, as a service to a government which does not know it needs it . . . is to deserve far more of history than we can give our guest tonight.

In some remarks preliminary to his address accepting the award, and in response to MacLeish, Paton said that although he did not feel worthy of it, he could not have refused it, "for the very announcement of it brought hope and encouragement to thousands of my fellow citizens in South Africa." And he went on: "Though you give this award to me, I feel, and many of them feel, that you are giving it to them. Many of them have had to pay for their beliefs and principles more dearly than I have been called upon to do; some of them spent a considerable part of this year in prison, arrested, detained and released without preferring any charge against them."[13]

Apart from these opening remarks, Paton made no futher reference to events in South Africa. He devoted the body of his address, in which he spoke as an African rather than a South African, to the problems of the African continent emerging from colonial rule, to race attitudes, and to the relations of the new African states to Western countries on the one hand and Communist states on the other. He pointed to three striking characteristics of the new Africa: the desire and determination to have freedom; the desire to walk as equals among the nations of the modern world; the bitter resentment against the arrogance of the color bar, a resentment that expresses itself in its extreme form as anti-Westernism.

In the course of his return journey to South Africa, Paton addressed some meetings in England to help raise money for Defence and Aid. He also attended the World Council of Churches meetings in Geneva, Switzerland. When he arrived at Johannesburg airport his passport was confiscated by government officials. An editorial in the *New York Times* hailed this act as "A New Honor for Alan Paton." The government-run South African Broadcasting Corporation bitterly attacked him for being unpatriotic, but refused to allow him to reply on its transmitters. Responding through the press, Paton said that he did not identify the Nationalists with South Africa, and that he did not regard it as unpatriotic to criticize them abroad. He interpreted the summary withdrawal of his passport as the penalty imposed by the Nationalists after twelve years in power for his having continued to say and write what he thought to be the truth. He was equally unrepentant in a letter to the cabinet minister who had ordered his passport withdrawn. He wrote: "I hope to have my passport returned in due course by a government fully representative of the people of South Africa."[14]

In 1970, after the Liberal party had been dissolved, and while Paton was engaged in research for his biography of Archbishop Clayton which required him to go to England, he applied for a passport on the grounds that it was necessary for his work as a writer, and he was given one.

Chapter Eight

An Exemplary Biography: *Hofmeyr*

The Afrikaner Liberal

For some years Paton's literary reputation rested on two successful novels and a handful of short stories. But the judgment of the future may rank his biographies of Jan Hofmeyr and Archbishop Geoffrey Clayton as well as his own autobiographical writings as a comparable literary achievement. With extended interruptions, Paton worked on his biography of Hofmeyr—a superb administrator under whose leadership white South Africans seemed inclined to move toward the goal of a common society—over a period of fifteen years, between Hofmeyr's death in December 1948 and the completion of the manuscript in March 1963. The plan for this book was in incubation for an even longer period. Paton wrote his first biographical sketch of Hofmeyr, "Jan Hendrik Hofmeyr—An Appreciation," in 1936,[1] and he records that at some time during World War II he told Hofmeyr that he would one day write his life. Hofmeyr, he adds, did not show great enthusiasm, but said: "I think you could."[2]

Jan Hofmeyr was first of all an intellectual prodigy. When he was only five years old it was discovered that he had taught himself to read in both English and Dutch, and that he could repeat verbatim the sermons he heard in church. He began school at the age of eight and completed the whole elementary and secondary curriculum within four years. At twelve he went on to the university, and at fifteen he received the B.A. with first-class honors. Such progress was spectacular but one-sided. He was intellectually superior to his classmates at the university, but in other aspects he was a mere child among adults, and his mother insisted that he dress as a child. He was therefore isolated from more mature fellow students, particularly in emotional or social attachments. Since his interest was solely in intellectual achievement, his other aptitudes were poorly developed, and all his life he lacked that quality "which responds to music or poetry or painting or drama." He also lacked interest in his personal appearance, and became notorious for the carelessness and untidiness of his dress.

Hofmeyr's father died when he was two years old. From that time on, his life became inextricably entwined with his mother's love and domination. Mrs. Hofmeyr loved her son fiercely and exclusively, and cared for him tirelessly. She was a forthright, outspoken, and strong-willed woman. Paton invariably describes her will in such terms as *indomitable*, *implacable*, and *imperious*: "Her will was implacable . . . one either capitulated to it or got out of her reach." She was also a devoutly religious woman with a strict puritanical spirit that weighed infidelity to moralities great or small in equal scale. Yet she enjoyed malicious gossip and was noted for her cutting tongue. Her love for her son was genuine, but she failed to distinguish between love and possessiveness. Hofmeyr soon learned that the price of his mother's devotion was his devotion; any attempt to break free "would create such crisis of recriminations, claims, self-pityings, and other ugliness, that he could not have borne it."

Hofmeyr never broke from his mother, but he did try to wean himself from her possessiveness and he gradually established an autonomous area—the realm of public affairs—where he was sole master. Otherwise they remained "inseparably joined together like Siamese twins of the spirit." The spirit of Mrs. Hofmeyr broods over Paton's biography in something like the same degree that she herself held sway over her son's life as she cared for him, yet was unreasonably jealous of his infinitesimal sallies toward other women. But in death the son finally parted from the mother under the cloud of her displeasure. In the last days of his life he disobeyed her—foolishly as it turned out—to undertake some minor duties when she felt that his poor health would not permit such activity. Paton emphasizes the drama of Hofmeyr's struggle to wean himself from his mother's possessive love, but he unfolds with even greater care the drama of Hofmeyr's struggle to emancipate his mind from white South African prejudices.

Paton believed that if he could write any life it would be Hofmeyr's. He knew Hofmeyr's home and his mother, and also something of the relationship that bound mother and son so closely. He had long shared Hofmeyr's interest in the work of the Students' Christian Association and he was familiar with the side of Hofmeyr's complex personality revealed at the annual boys' camps. But however well qualified Paton was to write a biography of Hofmeyr, the undertaking became, eventually, a most difficult and time-consuming task.

Reflecting on the reasons that may prevent a writer from regularly producing new works, Paton's fellow South African William Plomer remarked that the most important of these was life itself, which may "impose such duties, exert such stresses, or bring such fulfilments upon a writer that it absorbs those creative energies which might have been given to art."[3] Plomer's estimate fits Paton's case exactly. The success of *Cry, the Beloved Country*, and the interest it aroused, had encouraged Paton to devote his time to writing about South Africa. He therefore retired from the state service as principal of Diepkloof Reformatory in 1948; and he gave some of his reasons for doing so in a broadcast talk:

I have left the Public Service, but not with any intention of living in idleness or ease. I want to interpret South Africa honestly and without fear. I cannot think of any more important or exciting task. All my life, of course, I have lived actively in a world of problems and people, and I do not know if I shall be able to live the kind of life an author seems to find necessary. This is one of the things I must find out for myself.[4]

Paton was given little freedom from the world of problems. Even before the year 1948 had ended, Jan Hofmeyr died. His last injunction, whispered to his brother, was: "Tell my friends to carry on." Hofmeyr's death, on 3 December 1948, left the road ahead full of uncertainties for those who had hoped he would be the mainstay of the liberal cause in South Africa. Paton felt his death keenly. As a private man he could not "carry on" Hofmeyr's work in public affairs, but he was better qualified than others in Hofmeyr's circle to write his biography, and he immediately prepared to do so.

At first the work went well. In the early stages he lived with

Hofmeyr's mother, Mrs. Deborah Hofmeyr, then aged eighty-eight, and "learned the true version of many legends." But his reluctance to rely on her viewpoint alone, and his determination to ferret out others, whether friend or foe, familiar with Hofmeyr's career, displeased her. She took a violent dislike to the idea of a biography that proposed to explore her son's personality and be something more than a record of his public career. It became clear to Paton that the kind of biography he envisaged, particularly one that would "relate her own tremendous role in her son's life," could not be published while she was alive. So in 1952 he laid the work aside for the time being.

Mrs. Hofmeyr lived for seven years after they parted. When she died at the age of ninety-five on 27 July 1959, Paton took up the work again; but by then he admits he was "no longer a pure writer, having felt it a duty to follow Hofmeyr's course and collaborate with Margaret Ballinger, Leo Marquard, Jordan Ngubane, Peter Brown and others, in the work of the Liberal Party, founded in 1953." It took almost four more years of work to complete the book. During this time there were further interruptions, of which the most serious was the State of Emergency during 1960, when Peter Brown was imprisoned and Paton had to act as national chairman of the Liberal party. He refers to this time of trials in an essay, "The Hofmeyr Biography,"[5] but he omits mention of the fact that the unfinished manuscript of the biography "spent part of its life hidden lest police should raid and take it away."[6] (Paton's son Jonathan recalls that it was he who hid the manuscript—in a piano.)

An Inner Drama

Paton's life of Hofmeyr appeared first in South Africa where it was published by the Oxford University Press under the title *Hofmeyr* in 1964; and a somewhat abbreviated version, edited by Dudley C. Lunt, appeared the following year in New York under the title *South African Tragedy: The Life and Times of Jan Hofmeyr*.

Paton's *Hofmeyr* is, essentially, about the moral and intellectual development of a man whose lot was to become deputy prime minister for a time and afterwards to be rejected because of his liberal views on civil rights. Although Paton had been Hofmeyr's friend, and a great admirer of his moral courage, the biography was not persevered with through years of difficulties simply out of friendship or admiration. There were those who thought that "of all the lives waiting to be written, Hofmeyr's was the least promising—dull, virtuous, conventional, with no wine, women, or song." Paton, with a novelist's discernment, realized that on the contrary Hofmeyr's life had "an inner drama as exciting as anything to be found in South Africa."[7] This inner drama might have proved reason enough to undertake the work, but Paton had a more compelling reason. He was convinced that the story of Hofmeyr's life could reveal the true spirit of South Africa in our times more clearly than the biography of any other public figure, including Field Marshal Smuts.

Hofmeyr's biography does not assume this importance as a direct outcome of his personal qualities. Paton takes pains to point out that Hofmeyr's liberalism was characterized by cautious advances and conservative retreats, and that many of the categories of his thought bear little relevance to the realities of present day Africa.

Even had Hofmeyr never lived, the story of South Africa in our times would have been a story of conflicting views on whether increased freedom or more narrow restrictions should shape society in that multiracial land. Hofmeyr saw this conflict clearly, and stated it straightforwardly when he said in 1938 that "in the mind of the average white South African there was a struggle between the desire to be just and the fear of being just. Yet fear produces hatred and hatred produces disaster. Therefore one must go forward in faith not fear."[8] In 1946, in a commencement address at the University of the Witwatersrand, he appealed for the addition of a fifth freedom— freedom from prejudice—to the four freedoms of the Atlantic Charter. This address became known as Hofmeyr's *Herrenvolk* speech, because in a direct allusion to Nazi racism he declared, "The plain truth, whether we like it or not, is that the dominant mentality in South Africa is a *Herrenvolk* mentality." He went on to say that prejudice was South Africa's hallmark. He warned of its consequences for the country's economic progress and concluded:

But our chief loss is a moral loss. As long as we continue to apply a dual standard in South Africa to determine our attitudes towards . . . European and non-European on different ethical bases, to assign to Christian doctrine a significance which varies with the colour of a man's skin, we suffer as a nation from what Plato would have called the lie in the soul—and the curse of Iscariot may yet be our fate for our betrayal of the Christian doctrine which we profess.[9]

Hofmeyr's *Herrenvolk* speech also contained a warning against "the growing tendency to describe as Communist . . . any who asked for fair play for all races or who suggested that non-Europeans really should be treated as the equal of Europeans before the law." Yet only a few years after his death, this "tendency to describe" was translated into a tendency to proscribe under the Suppression of Communism Act broadly interpreted.

During the fifteen years of his South African parliamentary career, Hofmeyr became identified with the Spirit of Liberty. One aspect of his story significant for the world at large, therefore, lies not in the measure of how modest or how exemplary his liberalism was in practice, but in how the mere sight of it provoked the Spirit that Denies to fortify the citadel of racial intolerance. The political conflict that embroiled Hofmeyr had sensitive wellsprings running deeper than differences in social or political outlooks. Hofmeyr's belief that South Africa should aspire toward a common society recognizing the human significance of all men was based on his Christian convictions. But his parliamentary opponents—supporters of a political ideal which they called "Christian Nationalism"—differed radically from him in their conception of Christianity. Paton characterizes the more extreme among them as "outraged believers in that heretical Christianity which has made racial separation the highest of all goods, and racial difference a God-given gift which no ordinary man could set aside."

Because of this fundamental difference in outlook, the Nationalist party's clash with Hofmeyr attained the uncompromising intensity of a holy war, waged openly under the slogan provided by J. G. Strijdom, a later prime minister: "Hofmeyr must be destroyed." It is in this context that Hofmeyr's story, as Paton pointed out to Studs Terkel in an interview, becomes the story of out times:

Hofmeyr's story is *the* story of our times in South Africa—even more than the biography of Jan Smuts—because he not only tried to resist the drift to authoritarianism and neofascism but he proclaimed his Christian principles when it came to racial questions. Looking back from today one sees that Hofmeyr is very likely outdated—things move too fast—but that doesn't alter the fact that he was the obstacle to the realization of present policies. Hofmeyr was a minister in Smuts's government, and in any normal society he would have been his successor, but he couldn't because he split his own party with his views on racial affairs. The United Party feared that if Hofmeyr continued he would drive all the right wingers into the Nationalist Party and, although Hofmeyr died before that occurred, that is precisely what has happened: the right wing of the United Party was taken over by the Nationalists. [10]

Between Principle and Expediency

One of the principal dramatic themes of Paton's biography of Hofmeyr is the dilemma of the private man who must trim his personal ideals to the exigencies of public office. The crucial instance of this revolves about the question of why Hofmeyr did not found a Liberal party. The problem is a complex one, with bearings on his relationship to General Smuts, his relationship with other liberals, and his personal capacity for leadership; but at least part of the answer rests on the inescapable conclusion that some gains could be made within the framework of the United party, which held office, while none at all might be made by a splinter Liberal party out of office. Since Hofmeyr did not raise the liberal banner himself, the question of the depth and sincerity of his liberal commitment is unanswerable. But one can, perhaps, measure it in terms of a parallel instance of the difference between his private ideals and what he thought publicly expedient.

One reason why the humanitarian-minded were displeased with Hofmeyr's seeming parsimony in the area of African education while he was minister for finance was that they believed him to be very keenly interested in supporting education for Africans. The sums of public money he put aside for this did not seem to them in keeping with his reputation. Yet the cause of African education lay near Hofmeyr's heart, and if his public expenditures do not bear this out his private arrangements do.

Hofmeyr and his mother lived frugally all their lives. They even succeeded in saving a substantial sum from his Rhodes Scholarship money while at Oxford. Hofmeyr had no private means. He delayed his entry into politics until he thought he had saved enough from his salary to make him financially independent. Later, when he felt his savings would provide modestly for himself and his mother in their retirement, he established a private trust fund, which he called the Deo Gratias fund, to be used for the advancement of African education. Into this fund Hofmeyr paid four-fifths of his ministerial salary each year. And he made this sacrifice, as Paton puts it, "out of thanks to God for the mercies of his mother and his honours and his industrious life." After his death the money in this fund was handed over to the Jan Hofmeyr School of Social Work, started by the YMCA to open up social work as a profession for African men and women.

Over against this personal commitment there is the record of Hofmeyr's public achievement. Traditionally in South Africa, the education and welfare of the African population was financed by special taxes on Africans and not from the general revenue, which was thought of as "white tax money." Traditionally, too, per capita expenditures followed a discriminatory scale geared to the standard of living of each group. The public expenditure on each white child in school, for example, was approximately seven times greater than the expenditure on each African child.

The legislation affecting Africans that Hofmeyr introduced during his terms of office rejected one of these traditional principles but not the other. We have already seen in the discussion of the origin of Diepkloof Reformatory how the improvements introduced by his Children's Act of 1935 applied equally to children of all races. In subsequent years he introduced legislation financing education for African children out of the general revenue, and establishing the practice that money for African schools be distributed through the national Department of Education and not through the Department of Native Affairs. Again, when he introduced legislation involving change in old-age pensions and social-welfare benefits, he saw to it that these benefits were extended to all races, although he accepted the traditional discriminatory scale of payments.

In these respects Hofmeyr made gains toward establishing principles for a common society, but not toward equal social justice. The actual sums of money from the common budget expended on African education were small, partly because South Africa was on a wartime economy and partly because the opposition even within his own party would not permit him larger sums. The small practical gains caused Africans to doubt the sincerity of his liberal commitment, and this doubt seemed justified in view of another impasse that was painful for Hofmeyr. In 1946, while General Smuts was attending the United Nations meeting at Lake Success, it fell to Hofmeyr as acting prime minister to respond to the demands of the Natives' Representative Council for alleviating the effects of discriminatory laws. Hofmeyr had to refuse to accede to the council's demands even in the face of its determination to boycott subsequent sessions. Paton sees this event as a turning point in South African history. "After that, " he says, "the demand of non-white people was for equality, not alleviation. . . . And Hofmeyr, in the eyes of many non-white people, ceased to be the spokesman of freedom and became the spokesman for white supremacy. He knew it, and found it painful."

Paton's interest in the dilemma of a man of strong principles in an office of public trust has parallels in his creative writing. This dilemma supplies the essential theme of *Sponono*, and Paton has referred to the parallel in responding to a question about the play. Of the conflict between Sponono and the Principal he says, "Finally, the boy passes judgment on the man. What is involved is the difficulty of carrying out the Christian injunction to forgive until seventy times seven—especially when you are in a position of power and authority." Paton then goes on to draw the parallel with Hofmeyr:

Hofmeyr is a case in point: a man with great Christian principles he was also Deputy Prime Minister and had to go to our Natives' [Representative] Council here to tell them he could not remove discriminatory laws. I think we must accept the fact that the good private individual must behave somewhat differently when a public man. No use weeping over that. If you are going into politics and accept a position of power you must trim your sails. . . .[11]

South African Tragedy

Paton's *Hofmeyr* was published in the United States in October 1965 in a slightly abridged version with the title *South African*

Tragedy: The Life and Times of Jan Hofmeyr. This abridgment by Dudley C. Lunt reduces the original book of some 550 pages by about one-fifth. It adds an informative "Prefatory Note" and concluding "Editorial Note" which supply useful background information; but it omits the author's footnotes and concentrates his forty brief chapters into nineteen longer ones, conventionally titled, going from "The Early Years" to "The End of the Road." These changes may enhance the book for readers who approach it as a political chronicle of the times, and at least one reviewer whose orientation is political preferred this abridged version. But to the extent that it molds the biography into a chronicle, the abridgment detracts from its artistic effectiveness.

Even the decision to omit footnotes was taken at some cost to the integrity of the text. For example. Paton is concerned with the extent to which Hofmeyr's liberal views contributed to the disintegration of the United Party. He quotes the view of judge Leslie Blackwell that Hofmeyr's famous speech in 1936 opposing the curtailment of African voting rights precipitated the party split. Paton introduces this quotation with the statement, "It is interesting to read what Blackwell wrote about what he called 'this memorable speech.' " Judge Blackwell, as a distinguished national figure and as a friend of the Hofmeyr family, plays a role in the biography. His opinion on this important point bears greater weight than any anonymous opinion, yet, apparently to avoid a footnote reference to the source of the quotation, the text is changed to "It is interesting to read what one publicist wrote. . . ." The change is not only unnecessary, but meaningless, because what makes the quoted opinion *interesting* is that it was Blackwell's opinion. Again, for the sake of omitting the words "Mr. B. J. Vorster, in 1962," it seems hardly worth withholding the information that the author of the axiom, "Communism kills, but Liberalism leads one into ambush in order to kill," was the man soon to become Prime Minister of South Africa.

An abridgment must necessarily condense a text or omit portions of it. While, in general, this abridgment succeeds in its aim of presenting the substance of the biography in clear readable form, it unfortunately omits some details essential to the complete characterization of the man. For example, the account earlier in this chapter of Paton's interest in the drama of a public man's attempt to balance principle and expediency relies for a concrete instance on Hofmeyr's public and private disbursements on African education. The abridgment completely omits the account of the Trust Fund through which Hofmeyr donated four-fifths of his salary to African education. This deprives the reader of a significant insight into Hofmeyr's character and diminishes the inner drama on which the biography depends so much for its impact.

There can be no doubt that Paton saw the inner drama as of paramount importance. After completing the work he wrote an essay on his experience. In it he speaks of Hofmeyr's career as a subject for biography and comments: "As if these things were not enough for a biographic symphony, there were the two extraordinary relationships, not fully explicated because not fully explicable, of himself and his mother, and himself and Smuts. If such a symphony turned out to be dull, it would be only the composer who was to blame."[12] In *Hofmeyr*, Paton succeeds to a very high degree in attaining the completeness of a symphony.

Judged as a work of scholarship, Paton's biography has deficiencies. He is not meticulous about supplying exact references for source material, and he is overcareful in avoiding references to himself. His own name does not even appear in the index—although this may be a simple oversight. As a literary biography, however, it merits comparison with the best works in this genre. And Paton himself says in episode sixty-three of *For You Departed*, which describes the part his wife, Dorrie, took in the preparation of the book over many years: "So at last the stupendous task was finished. *Hofmeyr* was a book quite different from *Cry, the Beloved Country*, but in other respects I rank them as equal"(*FYD*, 139).

Chapter Nine

Apartheid and the Archbishop and *For You Departed*

An Anglican Bishop

Jan Hofmeyr died on 4 December 1948, five months after the defeat of his party by Dr. Malan's Nationalist party in May 1948. It was clear, even then, that the program to liberalize South Africa's racial laws envisioned by Hofmeyr and recommended by the Fagan Commission would remain stillborn. The Nationalist party had quickly set about enacting a series of parliamentary bills designed to separate the races of South Africa in every facet of their lives. Among the proposals subsequently enacted into law were the Prohibition of Mixed Marriages Act, 1949; the Population Registration Act, 1950 (which determined everyone's race); the Group Areas Act, 1950 (which determined racial areas for legal domicile and required the removal of residents not fitting the racial classification for which the area was designated).

Many such laws were enacted in subsequent years, including a special category of legislation that applied only to black Africans. These laws were the special province of the architect of *apartheid*, Dr. Hendrik Verwoerd, who later became prime minister. In 1957, Dr. Verwoerd brought forward his Native Laws Amendment Bill, of which Clause 29—commonly known as the Church Clause—seemed designed to prevent racially mixed congregations in places of worship. At a meeting in Cape Town in March of that year the Anglican bishops of South Africa drafted a letter to the prime minister, Mr. Strijdom, to tell him that if such a bill became law they would be unable to obey it or to counsel their clergy to obey it. The bishops appealed to the prime minister not to put them in the position of having to choose to obey conscience or the law of the land. This letter was set for signature before Dr. Geoffrey Clayton, Anglican Archbishop of Cape Town and Metropolitan of his church in South Africa. In signing it the archbishop performed the final act of his life; for having done so he suffered a heart seizure and died alone in his study. No representative of the state attended the archbishop's funeral; but his witness against *apartheid* is memorialized in Paton's second major biography, *Apartheid and the Archbishop: The Life and Times of Geoffrey Clayton, Archbishop of Cape Town* (1973).

Dr. Geoffrey Clayton had a distinguished career at Cambridge University and as Vicar of Chesterfield, England, before his installation as Bishop of Johannesburg in May 1934, the year before his fellow Anglican, Alan Paton, became principal of the city's penal institution for black youths, Diepkloof Reformatory. It was through an initiative of the new bishop of Johannesburg that Paton was soon to have one of his most important intellectual experiences. From 1941 to 1943 he was a member of the diocesan commission appointed by Bishop Clayton "to discover what it believed to be 'the mind of Christ for South Africa.'" In 1943 this commission presented to the Anglican Synod a report entitled *The Church and the Nation* which faced the problems of black wages and black poverty, of racial discrimination, and the extension of voting rights. His work on this commission convinced Paton that South African notions of white supremacy could not be reconciled with Christian principles: "As for myself, having lived for thirty-eight years in the dark, the Commission opened for me a door, and I went through into the light and I shut it against myself, and entered a new country whose very joys and adversities were made resplendent by the light" (117).

Paton regarded the Bishop of Johannesburg as the only person he knew whose intellect matched Jan Hofmeyr's; but despite this, the portrait he presents of him in *Apartheid and the Archbishop* is painted as Oliver Cromwell recommended, "warts and all"; and indeed the archbishop's warts and frailties served Paton's purpose so well that he may have been tempted to magnify them.

Clayton's physical appearance did not reflect his perfection of intellect. He had a large bald head, short legs, and a pot belly; and Paton represents him as both ungracious and ungainly. He loved his food and he ate immoderately and not elegantly. He smoked continuously. He would talk with a cigarette dangling from the corner of his mouth, spilling ash all over his stock and clothes. He was very irritable when he could not smoke—particularly during Lent, when he gave it up. Besides these temperamental quirks, Clayton, a life-long celibate, had an aversion to women, and his unease in their presence often expressed itself in rudeness; but he could be relaxed in the company of men, and he referred to this as his "nature." Paton says that his sexual code was strict, almost Puritanical; and that his "nature," like everything else about him—except smoking and his irritability—was fully controlled by his resolute will.

Clayton became a spiritual leader of the Anglican Church of the Province in South Africa—a church with more black members than white—when he was elected to the Archbishopric of Cape Town in November 1948, five months after the Nationalist party came to power with a commitment to implement *apartheid*. Schooled in respect for the law and in obedience to civil powers, Clayton did not seem cut out to be cast in a key role in the conflict between a multi-racial church and a racial state. While bishop of Johannesburg from 1934 to 1948 he had disapproved of those among his Anglican clergymen like the Reverends Michael Scott and Trevor Huddleston, who joined in active opposition to racial laws. Certainly, while he was bishop of Johannesburg, civil disobedience was unthinkable for Clayton who believed that his primary duty lay in pastoral care, not political activism. Yet, in 1952, during the sustained defiance campaign led by Chief Albert Luthuli and the African National Congress in which thousands of Africans took part, Clayton was beginning to address himself to the question of civil disobedience—a problem he wrestled with for the remainder of his life.

It seems likely that many biographers working on a life like that of Archbishop Clayton would highlight the church-state conflict and perhaps find parallels in T. S. Eliot's dramatic representation of Archbishop Thomas à Becket in *Murder in the Cathedral*. Paton deals with the theme of church-state conflict in some degree, but he also gives four additional themes their due emphasis: the strange person-ality of the archbishop; the spiritual and human affairs of the Church of the Province which he guided; the politics of the times in South Africa; and the incompatibility between the Calvinist Dutch Reformed Churches and other Christian churches in South Africa—particularly the Anglo-Catholic Church of the Province.

This broad historical approach immediately suggests that Paton regarded *Apartheid and the Archbishop* not as simply representing the drama of one life, but as a sequel in some sense to *Hofmeyr*, his biography of South Africa's leading liberal statesman of the era before *apartheid*. Paton's *Hofmeyr* was, as we have seen, the portrait of a public man striving to act politically in conformity with his Christian conscience. His *Apartheid and the Archbishop* is a portrait of a spiritual man reluctantly forced by his Christian perspective to act in the political sphere. The common quality that his subjects share, in Paton's representation, is their will to rise above personal limitations, prejudices, and parochial presuppositions and to move, however falteringly, toward the vision of a just multi-racial society. Clayton was installed as Archbishop of Cape Town three weeks before Hofmeyr's death in December 1948, and Paton is explicit in identifying him as the successor to Hofmeyr's moral leadership:

For the next eight years it was Clayton who was to be the defender of Christian liberal principle and practice. Ironically, he was to defend them against the new Christian Government, bearers of Protestant belief, and members of the Christian Church. He was going to comprehend more fully the vast and seemingly unbridgeable gulf that yawns between South African Calvinism and all the world's other churches. (170)

Because the Dutch Reformed Church to which the majority of Afrikaners belong is Calvinist, it is commonly thought that the racial attitudes embodied in *apartheid* have theological roots in the Calvinist doctrine of election. Paton counters this common assumption in two ways in *Apartheid and the Archbishop*: first, by direct, logical rebuttal; second, by the literary device of composing the entirety of *Apartheid and the Archbishop* as a parable—perhaps, more accurately, an allegory—of the Christian Way understood as an individual journey toward Isaiah's "holy mountain."

The thrust of Paton's direct logical rebuttal is that South African race prejudice is not directly derived from Calvinism: it has local historical origins; and insofar as South African Calvinists are racist, the source of their racism is to be found in their South Africanism rather than their Calvinism per se. That is the point, for example, in his statement about Clayton, in his South African experience, coming to comprehend more fully "the vast and seemingly unbridgeable gulf that yawns between South African Calvinism and all the world's other churches."

But *Apartheid and the Archbishop*, as a work of literature, shows that Paton's understanding of the theological issue goes much deeper than that; and for a clearer view we need to look again at his characterization of the archbishop. Paton presents him, despite his imperfections of personality, as a man whose spiritual strength has the support of considerable intellectual powers and a resolute will. He emphasizes the archbishop's control of self and his devotion to duty, and he also makes it quite clear that the archbishop is no romantic sentimentalist, no dreamer, no lover of beauty for its own sake.

The portrait we are given in *Apartheid and the Archbishop* is unquestionably that of a man of intellect and judgment who led the examined life, and whose mode of consciousness was a compound of will and resolve that was never allowed to dissolve into dream, mere wish, or fantasy. By contrast, the generality of white South African Anglicans, who formed only part of the Archbishop's flock, led "unexamined" lives and permitted themselves to identify what was expedient for retaining their privileged position in society with what morally ought to be. In Paton's view, a majority of white members of the Anglican church had fears and prejudices indistinguishable from those of their Calvinist fellow countrymen:

In synods all over South Africa it frequently happened that when discriminatory laws were debated, a majority of the white clergy and a minority of the white laity would join with the overwhelming majority of the black clergy and laity in condemning them. One can only suppose that many of the white laity had different values, different interests and felt that they had more to lose. (131)

Paton adds to this a significant passage giving his definition of a Christian. In it he speaks of "the never-ending struggle to the Christian to do what he believes to be right and not what is expedient, convenient, less frightening, more advantageous." In particular, he says of the Christian: "In him there should always be a tension between what he is, and what he aspires to be." And then the essential point: "This tension disappears in the hypothetical event that he becomes perfect." The normal state of the Christian is imperfection. Hence Paton's care with the wartiness of this portrait in which he sets the Archbishop before us with all his imperfections highlighted.

Having said that the tension disappears only in the hypothetical event that the Christian becomes perfect, Paton immediately speaks of a *pseudoperfection*—a perfection many white Christians in South Africa assume to be theirs simply by virtue of presumed racial superiority. The tension in the Christian, he says, "also disappears— or seems to disappear" when he is able to identify what suits his own convenience and advantage with what is right and just: "This is undoubtedly the solution achieved by many white Christians in South Africa, and one hesitates to contend that white Anglicans do not resort to it more than white Calvinists" (131).

The hypothetical state of perfection that Paton speaks of—the Holy Mountain of his autobiography—is a possibility open only to individuals and not to such collectives as races or nations. It seems Clayton at one time lacked discernment on this point. In his first pronouncement on race in Johannesburg in 1943, he quoted St. Paul: "Ye are all one in Christ Jesus," and continued:

But that does not mean that the Jew is the same as the Greek, and the male the same as the female. Neither is the European the same as the African. It is not that one is better than the other. When each race is brought to its perfection I believe the difference will persist. We are not going to be all alike in heaven. . . . (50)

Paton found the general tenor of this pronouncement questionable: "It almost seemed to be a foreshadowing of the doctrine of separate development." But the phrase "when each race is brought to its perfection" drew his strongest disapproval, and caused him to ask a whole catechism of questions:

Is any race ever brought to perfection? Cannot only persons be brought to perfection . . . ? Can one see anywhere signs of a race that has been brought to perfection? Or of a race in the process of coming to perfection? Is it not an impossible goal, which, when pursued in a multi-racial society by a ruling race, can cause great suffering to those races that are ruled? (51)

Paton's questions imply that utopian goals bring great suffering to those whose rulers deny them a voice in their own government. And, indeed, this implication would seem self-evident in a century that has witnessed the misery wrought by a variety of utopian political schemes under Stalin, Hitler, and their kind. Aleksandr Solzhenitsyn, a writer of comparable cast of mind to Paton's, probes the problem of suffering in *The Gulag Archipelago*. "To do evil," says Solzhenitsyn, "a human being must first of all believe that what he is doing is good." Solzhenitsyn finds that our appetite for evil in this century has crossed a *threshold magnitude* (like the 183 degrees at which oxygen liquefies); and that to our contemporary perception classical evildoers like Shakespeare's Macbeth, or Iago, seem farcical and clumsy. Solzhenitsyn says that Shakespeare's evildoers "stopped short at a dozen corpses"—because they had "no *ideology*" to supply their evildoing with justification. He says that agents of the Inquisition fortified their wills "by invoking Christianity; the conquerers of foreign lands, by extolling the grandeur of the Motherland; the colonizers, by extolling Civilization; the Nazis, by race; the Jacobins (early and late), by equality, brotherhood, and the happiness of future generations.' And he adds, "Thanks to *Ideology*, the twentieth century was fated to experience evildoing on a scale calculated in the millions."[1]

In his autobiography *Towards the Mountain*, Paton expresses himself in terms that resemble Solzhenitsyn's when he says of the advent to power of the Afrikaner Nationalist party under Dr. Malan in 1948:

It was a new era that had begun. The task before the new government was nothing less than to fashion not only the perfect society, but one which should endure into foreseeable time, one in which every race would be allotted its place and function. . . . So noble was the end . . . so sublime the goal, that almost any means became justifiable. (*TM*, 309)

Set against a background of contrast between inhuman aims of utopian ideologies and the individual human journey or Pilgrim

Way, Paton's portrait of the archbishop, graceless, ungracious, bad-tempered, more than a little spiteful, delighting in malicious gossip, and with disconcerting habits, is the portrait of a potential Christian who has to work at the business of becoming a Christian. As a struggling pilgrim still on the way, his state is an ironic commentary on those, smugly satisfied with the pseudoperfection of racial superiority, who assume that, for whites only, Paradise was not really lost and does not have to be regained. In Paton's handling of biography as a literary mode, therefore, Archbishop Clayton becomes something more that an historical figure. The story of his life becomes an allegory of the Christian way—a South African *Pilgrim's Progress*—an allegorical journey of the kind undertaken also by many of the characters in Paton's novels and biographies.

Consequently, besides its themes of Church, State, and Race, and the Archbishop's personal pilgrimage, *Apartheid and the Archbishop* is of interest for what it reveals of the mind of Alan Paton, by affording a fresh perspective on themes consistently present in his work from the beginning. As noted in Chapter 1, one characteristic of Paton's way of seeing the world is the pervasive allegory of the Pilgrim Way—the coming out from various forms of darkness and ignorance into the light by which the exemplary characters in his works of fiction attempt to become something they were not before.

Reviewing *Apartheid and the Archbishop* in the *New York Times* Edward B. Fiske summed up its embodiment of Paton's perspective:

> One cannot escape the conclusion that at his best Dr. Clayton expresses the values that have sustained Mr. Paton himself in his long witness against *apartheid*. . . . The last chapter . . . notes that the racial problem in South Africa is as serious now as it was in Dr. Clayton's time, and he asks whether this brilliant and crusty churchman really achieved anything at all in his . . . years as an Archbishop. His answer, in effect, is that a Christian is called to be faithful, not successful, and therein lies not only a goal for human existence but a resource for pursuing it.[2]

For You Departed: An Intimate Memorial

Paton had earlier taken up the theme of the Pilgrim Way in *For You Departed* (1969)—his memorial for his first wife, Dorrie Francis. This book was initially published in London as *Kontakion for You Departed*, a title drawn from the climactic passage: "And this book is done too, this Kontakion for you departed . . . it is a strange story and now it is done." A kontakion is an early Byzantine liturgical chant, elaborately composed of stanzas and linking refrains, performed (like a *Te Deum* in the Western church) to celebrate some public event or deliverance. Paton had in mind a particular kontakion that had a place in family memories: the Russian Orthodox "Kontakion for the Departed," sometimes spoken of as "the Kief Kontakion" or the "Kief Melody," which is quoted in full in the text.

This kontakion used to be sung as part of the annual Memorial Day services by the choir of St. John's College, Johannesburg, where Paton's sons David and Jonathan went to school. Jonathan Paton remembers that his parents frequently attended this annual service, and that his father was especially moved by the beauty of the Russian Kontakion. He owned a phonograph record of the St. John's choir Memorial Day service, and in replaying it after his wife's death, Paton found great comfort in the words of the song, which oppose to the pain of sorrow the affirmative words of rejoicing.

For You Departed is composed of sixty-nine numbered passages varying in length from a few lines to several pages arranged antipho-nally: passages set in the immediate present—at the time of his wife's death—alternate with passages that flash back in time to their earlier life. Dorrie Paton died in 1967, the year the Liberal party was dissolved in the face of the enactment of legislation making it illegal. Consequently Paton's literary method of moving backward and forward in time sets the events of their lives against a worsening climate of race relations in South Africa.

Paton starts with the early morning of his wife's death and the immediate task of the living: "I prayed may her soul rest in peace. I did not weep. I set about the business of preparing your funeral." The succeeding odd-numbered episodes recount the experiences of the funeral, unusual in segregated South Africa: "There was the church itself packed with people of all the nations under our sun, just the kind of company you would have wished to be about you. . . . There were many there who mourned for you, but it was above all else a service of thanksgiving . . . the most wonderful funeral service I ever attended" (14—15).

Episode "Two," the first of the memories evoked, recalls their
initial meeting on the tennis courts at Ixopo in 1925: she a woman
married to a man in the final stages of tuberculosis, but full of zest,
laughter, mischief, and a touch of coquetry, who, emancipated for
those days, smoked cigarettes and did not object to liquor; and he "a
shy clear-eyed virgin" brought up among Christadelphians in a home
where liquor was prohibited and the belief that women should not
smoke "enjoyed almost the status of an article of faith."

Thereafter the even-numbered passages move forward in chrono-
logical time starting with the joy and pain of young complicated
love—"the halcyon days." The odd-numbered passages remain in the
present throughout. This antiphonal arrangement produces a deliberate opposition, or counterpointing, so that in its artistic form the
book embodies its homiletic theme: while yesterdays may be recalled, they cannot be relived. This is a clear warning against the
temptation to seek some Edenic or Arcadian past, a desire that can
become a morbid growth in nations that deify the past.

For You Departed was first made public when Paton read substantial
portions of it in Rhodes University Theatre on 8 July 1969. Before
beginning, he explained: "This document is a very intimate one;
nevertheless I will read portions of it, because I think as you get older
you don't wish to keep intimate things so close to yourself as you did
when you were young." As he began to read there was silence in the
crowded auditorium—not just the usual cessation of rumblings, but
the silence of embarrassed disbelief at the intimate revelations unfolding before them in staccato, yet austere, musical rhythms. Gradually,
as the work's range of mood, humor, and movement emerged, there
were stirrings of laughter at witty anecdotes followed by repeated wholehearted bursts of laughter during the reading of episode
"Thirty"—a highly amusing narrative about a family card game at
Diepkloof called Reformatory Bridge. The stillness returned as he
read of detentions, house arrests, and searchings by the security
police, but the sanity of humor pervaded even these somber recitals.

He told, for example, about a statement he had written for the
press in anticipation of being arrested the day he was to fly to
Swaziland to visit Bishop Reeves, formerly the Anglican bishop of

Johannesburg, who had taken refuge there in 1962. He reminisced to his departed wife:

No one came that day to arrest me and when I left at dusk I gave the document into your safe-keeping. You hid it on top of one of the cupboards in the guest bathroom, but as you lay in bed it became oppressively clear to you that when the security police came, they would go straight to the top of the cupboards in the guest bathroom. So you took it down from there and put it into your rolled-up red-and-white umbrella hanging in your dressing room. Then back in bed it became equally clear to you that when the police came, they would go straight to your red-and-white umbrella hanging in the dressing room. Then you had an inspiration of genius (which admittedly was based on the assumption that the security police were all gentlemen), and you took the document and taped it to your stomach, and then got back into bed. (136)

Of the statement that his wife so anxiously concealed, Paton said in *For You Departed*: "It was one of the best things I ever wrote because I always write better under the influence of emotion. I don't know where it is now, but if I find it, it will go into this book." He did not find it then, for it does not appear in *For You Departed*. But it was subsequently published in *Knocking on the Door* with the title, "Under Threat of Arrest."

The problem of suffering and its acceptance is also the subject of other works Paton wrote about the same time as *For You Departed*—works that examine this profound subject in wider contexts than those of personal or South African experience. These works include "Why Suffering," his contribution to the symposium *Creative Suffering: The Ripple of Hope* (Philadelphia, 1970); "The Challenge of Fear," his contribution to the *Saturday Review* book *What I Have Learned: A Collection of Autobiographical Essays by Great Contemporaries* (New York, 1968); and *Instrument of Thy Peace* (New York, 1968)—a book of Lenten meditations prompted by the prayer of St. Francis of Assisi: "Lord, make me an instrument of Thy peace." In his "Prologue" to the last named, Paton says: "This book was written for sinners by one of them"; and he adds: "I write also for those who are inclined to be melancholy, for those who are inclined to withdraw rather than participate, for those who are tempted to keep some, or most, or all, of their love and pity for themselves" (7). Reviewing this book for the *New York Times Book Review*, Robert F. Capon compared it to Dag Hammarskjold's spiritual diary: "Like Hammarskjold's *Markings* (from which it quotes), it gives us a glimpse of the personal roots out of which great public performances spring"; and he further characterizes the book as "a severely gentle condemnation of melancholy and despair."[3]

Paton had had earlier occasion to warn his coworkers in the Liberal party against melancholy and despair. Addressing the last legal multiracial protest meeting to be held in Johannesburg, on 24 April 1968, he recalled what he had said to the remnants of the party in 1965 after some forty of its leaders had been banned:

Stand firm by what you believe; do not tax yourself beyond endurance, yet calculate clearly and coldly how much endurance you have; don't waste your breath and corrupt your character by cursing your rulers and the South African Broadcasting Corporation; don't become obsessed with them; keep your friendships alive and warm, especially with people of other races; beware of melancholy and resist it actively if it assails you; And give thanks for the courage of others in this fear-ridden country. (*LV*, 251)

In *For You Departed* he writes eloquently of his wife's courage in the face of attacks on the Liberal party:

Where did your courage come from? It was your religion of course, that strange Christianity of yours that took seriously the story of the Cross, that understood with perfect clarity that one might have to suffer for doing what one thought was right, that rejected absolutely the kind of Crossless geniality that calls itself Christianity. (145)

It may be said of Paton's writings taken as a whole that their characteristic theme is the giving of thanks for the courage of others. Although deeply touched by personal emotion, *For You Departed* is less a cry of grief on the occasion of his wife's death than a thanksgiving for her courage in the often painful journey out from a relatively comfortable life among white South Africans in Ixopo and Pietermaritzburg to the unfamiliar prison world of Diepkloof, the uncertain world of a teacher turned writer in middle age, and the fearful world of anti-*apartheid* politics in the Liberal party. Finally it gives thanks for her courage to endure her final painful illness. His two major biographies, those of Jan Hofmeyr and Archbishop Clayton, are essentially tributes to men of courage in a fear-ridden country. His preface to *Cry, the Beloved Country* includes a tribute to the courage of Alfred Hoernlè, president of the Institute of Race Relations, whom he identifies as "Prince of Kafferboeties," so turning a spiteful term of reproach (meaning *nigger-lovers*) into lyrical praise.

Many of Paton's "Long View" articles are also direct tributes to the courage of others: Margaret Ballinger (*LV*, 159–62), Elliot Mugadi (*LV*, 203–205), Bishop Trevor Huddleston (*LV*, 163–66), Peter Brown (*LV*, 210–12), and Chief Albert Luthuli (*LV*, 201–202). Furthermore, his autobiography measures milestones in his journey "Towards the Mountain" by examples of the courage of others. Here again, in *Towards the Mountain*, we encounter the example of the courageous public lives of Jan Hofmeyr, Alfred Hoernlè, and Archbishop Clayton. But there are examples of courage from more private lives, too: Edith Rheinallt Jones, whose courage and simple gift for nonracial friendships earned the love of people of all races so that they overflowed the church at her funeral service—an occasion that provided Paton with "the deepest experience" of his life (*TM*, 253); and Railton Dent, a college friend of whom Paton says in *Towards the Mountain*: "He taught me one thing, the theme of which will run right through this book, with undertones (or overtones, I never know which) of victories, defeats, resolutions, betrayals, that life must be used in the service of a cause greater than oneself" (59).

Chapter Ten

The 1980s:
No Marching to Utopia

Towards the Mountain

The first volume of Alan Paton's autobiography *Towards the Mountain*, published in 1980 when he was aged seventy-seven, brings the story of his private and public life to 1948. That crucial year, his forty-fifth, saw the publication of his first novel, *Cry, the Beloved Country*; his resignation from the principalship of Diepkloof Reformatory, a prison farm for black youths, which he had successfully transformed into a training school; and the accession to power in South Africa of the Afrikaner Nationalist party on a platform of "Christian Nationalism" which identified the will of God with white supremacy. To the extent that it is a record of Paton's delight in nature as a child, his love of books in boyhood, his later schooling, professional training, marriage, and reformatory work, we have already discussed *Towards the Mountain* in earlier chapters. But something remains to be said about the intellectual perspectives of this book, particularly its philosophical outlook and theological standpoint.

Towards the Mountain takes its title from Isaiah's vision of ineffable justice—when the lion will lie down with the lamb—"where they shall not hurt or destroy in all that holy mountain." The title, therefore, makes an implicit theological point also evident in *Apartheid and the Archbishop*: whereas individual souls may aspire toward a vision of perfect order out of reach in time, timebound collectives—the nations or races of the earthly city—cannot attain such perfection. The belief that they can is a utopian delusion.

Therefore, besides serving as a record of his boyhood, education, and early professional work, Paton's autobiography may be regarded as a criticism of authoritarian and closed utopian societies, for it tells how three separate utopian visions—each marked by a measure of authoritarianism, undue constraint, or injustice—touched on his life. The first such vision was that of the Christadelphians, the fundamentalist sect in which he grew up. Its members were law-abiding and uncompromisingly pacifist; but they forbade marriage with outsiders, regarded themselves as an elect, and looked forward to an earthly millennium when the worthy would enter the Kingdom.

In his university days Paton separated himself from the Christadelphians and joined Methodist friends in the Students' Christian Association; and later, as a teacher, he was active in YMCA, TOC-H, and related religious movements. He was then sought out by the Oxford Group, a moral reform movement seeking to establish itself in South Africa. "Its aim," says Paton, "was utopian, nothing less than the salvation of the human race. For this reason it selected key men and women for its targets, for if they were reconverted, their countries would turn to the ways of righteousness and peace." Their relentless pursuit, which reminded him of Francis Thompson's "The Hound of Heaven," deterred him from joining the Oxford Group. (Paton assumes his readers are familiar with Thompson's poem which envisions the Savior as the pursuing Hound of Heaven, beginning: "I fled him down the nights and down the days," and continuing, through elaborate stanzas, with variations on the refrain, "Still with unhurrying chase,/ And unperturbèd pace,/ Deliberate speed, majestic instancy,/ Come on the following Feet. . . .") And he says of the Oxford Group: "I knew that if the hunters caught me they would love me. I knew that if they did not catch me they would love me but not much" (122). He says he later found a matching relentlessness in the South African Security Police: "They have the same inexorability of purpose, the same intensity of gaze. They are hunting too, but if they catch you it will not be to love you" (122).

Paton was constantly accompanied by the Security Police when he was president of the Liberal party in the 1960s—a theme treated in *For You Departed*. But that is not part of the story of *Towards the Mountain*, which traces the rise of Afrikaner Christian nationalism only to the 1948 election victory, the prelude to an era in which "a new breed of Afrikaners were going to make fierce laws to achieve utopian purposes." The utopian task the new government set itself, says Paton, was "nothing less than to fashion not only the perfect society, but one which would endure into foreseeable time, one in which every race would be allotted its place and its function. . . . So noble was the end . . . so sublime the goal, that almost any means became justifiable. The Christian rulers of Afrikanerdom began to observe the unChristian precept that the end justifies the means" (309—10).

The vision of the perfect, enduring society is, of course, utopian, and attempts to actualize such visions in the present are invariably cruel. Only a finished work of art can objectify the absolute harmony, the reconciliation of contradictions, the subordination of detail to the whole, that characterize a perfected state of being; and as W. H. Auden says in *The Dyer's Hand*, where he draws such an analogy: "A society which was really like a good poem embodying the aesthetic virtues of beauty, order, economy, and subordination of detail to the whole, would be a nightmare of horror."[1]

Paton came to the writing of *Towards the Mountain* with a clear perception of the ways in which utopian *apartheid* constitutes a challenge to Christian principles; for this book was his third major essay in biography set against the historical background of the rise of Afrikaner nationalism. The first of these was *A South African Tragedy: The Life and Times of Jan Hofmeyr* (1964)—the biography of the wartime deputy prime minister. The second was *Apartheid and the Archbishop* (1973)—the life of Geoffrey Clayton, Anglican archbishop of Cape Town, who was reluctantly but steadily drawn to act in the political sphere. Both biographies show Paton's interest in the successive stages of spiritual growth that brought his subjects out from the confines of clichéd thinking and received opinions to the examined life; and, almost inevitably, into conflict with the rigidity of the *apartheid* mentality. His biographical method requires, therefore, simultaneous consideration of private and public life.

This is the method he employs also in *Towards the Mountain*; but it is a method that may militate against reducing the private and public events of the second half of his life to the compactness of the single volume referred to in a *New York Times* review by Thomas Pakenham: "The second volume . . . will carry him to the present. I think the best—and most harrowing—part of his 77-year trek is still to come."

Pakenham, author of the brilliant historical study *The Boer War* (1979), picks up Paton's term of praise for Alfred Hoernlé, "the Prince of Kafferboeties," and applies it to Paton: "Today, at seventy-seven, he is himself the Prince of Kafferboeties. For thirty years he has been the champion of the oppressed—and a thorn in the conscience of the Nationalists. No one alive has done more to interpret black and white South Africa to the world outside: its terrible wealth and beauty, its frustration and anguish and hope."[2]

In aptly summing up the qualities of Paton's life, Pakenham nevertheless overlooks two pertinent concerns: first, the problem of an appropriate autobiographical form for the anticipated volume that would reflect the political pressures and the unfolding drama of race relations in South Africa since 1948. As we have seen in this study, Paton best conveys his vision with the aid of such devices as parable and allegory, and through the use of fictional and dramatic forms. These forms admit a greater power of amplification than conventional biographical narrative and may best suit events of the second half of Paton's life.

In his summation, Pakenham also says, as so many others have done (including spokesmen for the South African government), that Paton interprets South Africa "to the world outside." Such remarks, although true of the widely read novels, obscure that fact that Paton's primary objective from the beginning was to open the eyes of his fellow white South Africans to the realities of their situation—hence the amount of time he devoted to the biographies of South African figures like Jan Hofmeyr and Bishop Clayton, and to writing articles and editorials for the journals *Contact* and *Reality*, and for local magazines and newpapers. Some of these occasional writings have been brought together in two collections. One of these, *The Long View* (1968), was discussed in Chapter 7. The other, the more recent collection *Knocking on the Door* (1975), edited by Colin Gardner, is a more representative selection of shorter works from Paton's earliest writing through the 1970s.

To Interpret South Africa Honestly

In *Knocking on the Door*, Colin Gardner has assembled Alan Paton's shorter writings that were either previously unpublished or had limited local circulation. His selection includes short fiction, verse, articles, and addresses, chronologically arranged over a span of fifty years, from September 1923, when Paton was a university student, until September 1974, when, at seventy-one, he was still vigorously championing racial justice in South Africa. Gardner's arrangement enables us to see Paton as a man of consistent vision and integrity who has sought by every available means—as a practical penal reformer; as a novelist, biographer, and poet; and as a public speaker denied conventional political platforms—to convince his fellow South Africans that society has more to gain from freedom freely offered than from freedom denied, with its attendant prohibitions, prison bars, and iron laws.

Content to let Paton's writing speak for itself, Gardner has confined his editorial interventions to a few lines of biographical information introducing each of the book's four sections, brief notes on publication, and a glossary of South African terms. (He distinguishes between the creative modes—verse and fiction—and other forms of discourse simply by setting the titles in italic or roman type.) The book is nevertheless a kind of surrogate biography.

Part One, with writings from 1923 to 1948, contains early poems and Paton's writings on penal reform, of which one in particular, "Freedom as a Reformatory Instrument," continues to bring the refreshing discovery that the title means precisely what it says. Part Two covers the years 1948 to 1953, a period after the reception of *Cry, the Beloved Country* when Paton sought :o devote himself to creative writing. This section contains, for the most part, short fiction and poetry. Part Three, 1953 to 1968, covers the fifteen years of Paton's involvement with the Liberal party, but confines the choice to fiction and discourse not collected in *The Long View*. It contains two of the half-dozen essays on literature to be found in the collection as a whole: "The South African Novel in English" and "Some Thoughts on the Contemporary Novel in Afrikaans." It also contains a short story, "Sunlight in Trebizond Street"—a Kafkaesque piece on a prisoner under police inquisition in some nameless, timeless place that may have been written in 1966 but was rejected shortly thereafter by a South African newspaper, no doubt for fear of censorship. The story was published in *South African Outlook* in 1970. Reviewing *Knocking on the Door* for the South African journal *Reality*, Tony Voss wondered if Paton had this story in mind in his interview with the *New York Times* in 1966 in which the interviewer states:

What Mr. Paton says he would like to do now is "to write a story of 1964"—the blundering efforts at sabotage by young activists, their imprisonments, the interrogations, the treachery of their friends, the trial, long sentences and the broken relationships that resulted.[3]

The point about 1964 particularly merits noting here because Paton developed some of this material about the blundering young activists in his account of "Lester" in *For You Departed* as well as in "Sunlight on Trebizond Street," and also because the story of the events of the 1960s necessarily forms much of the background of Paton's projected trilogy beginning with *Ah, But Your Land Is Beautiful* (1981). Some of the other matter in Part IV of *Knocking on the Door* also provides useful background for the period of this later trilogy. Part IV also includes one of Paton's most successful essays in autobiography, "The Case History of Pinkey" (1971), which skillfully and humorously combines barbed satire against *apartheid*—and other extremes of color consciousness—with an honest, if modest, appraisal of his own journey out from conventional white South African assumptions toward a nonracial outlook.

Another piece from recent years, "Memorial to Luthuli," an address delivered on the occasion of the unveiling of a tombstone at the grave of Chief Albert Luthuli in July 1972, is notable for two reasons: it justifies the title, *Knocking on the Door*, for this volume; and it exemplifies a local idiom, or mode of discourse, developed in response to the prohibitions of *apartheid* in which parable speaks more eloquently than the lie direct.

In his "Memorial to Luthuli," delivered on a Zululand hillside and translated by an interpreter for his largely Zulu audience, Paton recalled Franz Kafka's parable *The Trial*: "A man from the country comes to the city to look for justice. He goes to where justice should be, to the court of law. He knocks on the door but the doorkeeper will not open for him. There he sits day after day, month after month, year after year. And he goes on knocking on the door. But it is never opened for him." The metaphor of a man knocking on the door is, of course, a commonplace, and Paton did not have to go to Kafka for his instance. Chief Luthuli had applied the metaphor of knocking patiently on a closed door to himself and his opposition to *apartheid* twenty years before in response to his dismissal from the position of chief of the Groutville Mission Reserve in November 1952.

Those gathered at Luthuli's graveside would no doubt be aware that Paton drew on Kafka's parable because it is a crime in South Africa to quote any words of a person "banned," as Luthuli had been for the last fifteen years of his life. Instead, therefore, of quoting Luthuli's metaphorical remarks directly, Paton conjured up the memory of this arbitrary restriction the more effectively by seeming to respect the law: "He used to say—but of course the law says I cannot tell you what he used to say, although he has been gone from us those five years— and so I shall tell you what he used to believe." In doing so, Paton also recalled the first of his own "Long View" articles of fourteen years before (quoted in Chapter 7) where he related the parable: "I went to my brother and said, 'Brother, a man is knocking at the door.' My brother said, 'Is he a friend or an enemy?' I said to my brother, 'I have asked him and he says you will not know . . . until you have opened the door. . . . But if you do not open the door, you can be sure what he will be' " (*LV*, 135).

To some readers this may seem an overworking of a rather trite metaphor, but the element of repetition—particularly when the remarks were rendered into Zulu—would no doubt further recall for some hearers not only Luthuli's dedication to the cause of nonviolent resistance, but also the Zulu language protest song popular during the African National Congress defiance of unjust laws campaign of 1952. This song began with the line, "Open, Malan, we are knocking," repeated four times, followed by the twice repeated, "Wake up, Luthuli, Luthuli of Africa." It is not necessary that Paton should have intended to evoke all of this; for a parable takes on a life of its own that no amount of censorship or security can confine; and, if its allusions are local, it exerts greater power on those who share a life experience than on those outside looking in.

Much of Paton's writing is intentionally directed in this way for home consumption, not for export, as, for the most part, were the biographies to which he devoted so many years, *Hofmeyr* and *Apartheid and the Archbishop*, and the articles from the Liberal party journal *Contact*, collected in *The Long View*. His primary purpose as a writer has remained what he declared it to be when he resigned his post as principal of Diepkloof Reformatory in 1948: "I want to interpret South Africa honestly and without fear."

Ah, But Your Land Is Beautiful

Towards the Mountain, which brought the story of Paton's life to the publication of *Cry, the Beloved Country* in 1948 at age forty-five, may turn out to be one of the many autobiographies of the first half of a writer's life not followed by a continuation in kind. Such first biographies are more often the rule than the exception. Among the more famous are St. Augustine's *Confessions*, which covers his first thirty-three years—the traditional measure of a generation; Wordsworth's *Prelude*, which brings the writer to age twenty-eight; and Goethe's *Poetry and Truth*, which stops at age twenty-six. Remarking on this tendency, John S. Dunne quotes lines from W. B. Yeats's "A Dialogue of Self and Soul" and remarks: "The problem of the first generation of a man's life is the problem of what Yeats called 'the unfinished man in his pain,' while the problem of the second half is that of what he called 'the finished man among his enemies.' "[4] Early autobiography—that of "the unfinished man in his pain"—like Yeats's own *Reveries Over Childhood and Youth*—fits easily with the Romantic tradition of the past two centuries and with conventional narrative biographical forms. Later autobiography—that of "the finished man among his enemies"—must, perhaps, seek forms other than narrative capable of sustaining more powerful forces and pressures.

The problem of the differing requirements of autobiography, early and late, may have faced Alan Paton when, having completed his first autobiographical volume, *Towards the Mountain*, he set about writing its sequel. Going over the materials of the later period of his life—the period devoted to the work of the Liberal party—he may have found that the demands his material made on him were more appropriately met by fictional forms. He decided therefore to postpone work on his second volume of autobiography—the period of "the finished man among his enemies"—until he had first molded it imaginatively into a fictional trilogy beginning with *Ah, But Your Land Is Beautiful*—a title which implies a painful irony suspended between the hesitant *Ah, But*, and the conventional tourist compliment to South African residents: *Your Land Is Beautiful*.

As noted in Chapter 3, the passage in *Cry, the Beloved Country* that gave that book its title also indirectly supplies the title for the later novel. The passage in question begins, "Cry, the beloved country, for the unborn child that is the inheritor of our fear. Let him not love the earth too deeply. Let him not laugh too gladly when the water runs through his fingers. . . . For fear will rob him of all if he gives too much." Commenting on this passage in *Towards the Mountain* Paton says: "One does not really wish that a child should not love the earth too deeply but one is suggesting that if he loves it too deeply he cannot ask immunity from pain." And he adds: "That is what the visitors from America and Britain and Germany and other countries mean when they say to me, 'Ah, but your country is beautiful.' They mean, 'But why is it so full of pain.'" He says further that when he remembers that the passage in *Cry, the Beloved Country* was written in 1946 he is astonished that it took so many white people in South Africa thirty years to acknowledge its truth, "when black school-children started rioting in the great black city of Soweto on June 16, 1976, on the day after which, of all the hundred thousand days of our written history, nothing would be the same again" (*TM*, 293).

The subject matter of Paton's trilogy beginning with *Ah, But Your Land Is Beautiful* is the period between 1948 and 1976, dominated politically in South Africa first by Dr. Hendrik Verwoerd, framer of the racial ideology of *apartheid*, and later by Prime Minister J. B. Vorster, framer of the code of laws that made almost any expression of opposition to apartheid illegal. Since both held cabinet rank in the administrations of Prime Ministers D. F. Malan (1948–52) and Johannes Strijdom (1952–58), their fictional counterparts are shadowy background presences in *Ah, But Your Land Is Beautiful*.

This first novel in Paton's projected trilogy begins with the launching of the nonviolent defiance campaign in June 1952 by the Indian and African Congresses. It ends with the inauguration of Dr. Hendrik Verwoerd as Prime Minister in September 1958. In its blend of fictional and historical matter this novel resembles Leon Uris's *Trinity*, in which three fictional Irish families live out their lives against a background of the events of Irish history between the 1840s and the Easter Rising of 1916. Paton's novel is more compressed and faster paced—it is about one-third the length of *Trinity*—and it is in a curious way more joyful. Yet, whereas Uris drew his knowledge of Irish history from the detached narrative of school textbooks, Paton lived through the events he writes about.

One of Paton's characters—the Liberal party leader Robert Mansfield—is a partial self-portrait. Some of the other characters including Chief Luthuli and Patrick Duncan are real persons who appear under their own names. Others are wholly fictional. Among these is Van Onselen, a senior civil servant in the office of the Minister of Justice who supports the adminstration's plans for the separation of the races as fervently as Robert Mansfield and his friends oppose them. Van Onselen admires the statecraft of Dr. Hendrik—the thinly disguised fictional counterpart of Dr. Hendrik Verwoerd—and he looks forward to the realization of Dr. Hendrik's utopian ideal when the total separation of the races will permit each race to sustain its "God-given identity." In frequent letters to his aunt he confides his anticipation of "a Golden Age" by 1976—the year, ironically, when the black schoolchildren of Soweto rose in revolt against the system of Bantu Education that Dr. Verwoerd had imposed on them.

Ah, But Your Land Is Beautiful is not a plotted novel in the conventional sense. It is arranged in five main episodes—analogous to the five acts of a drama—and it has a brief epilogue which is at the same time a prologue foreshadowing the concerns to be taken up in the second work of the proposed trilogy. The subtitles of the five major episodes are "The Defiance Campaign," "The Cleft Stick," "Come Back, Africa," "Death of a Traitor," and "The Holy Church of Zion." The Epilogue is titled "Into the Golden Age."

The opening of the "The Defiance Campaign" is superbly done. It rivals the best moments in Paton's earlier fiction. In it a young Indian girl, Prem Bodasingh, the only child of wealthy parents, goes to jail repeatedly for repeating the offense of entering a library reserved for whites. Similar foreground scenes in other episodes reveal the effect of *apartheid* laws on individual lives: the removal of black residents from areas designated for whites only; the fate of a man of mixed blood who has married a white woman and attained some seniority in a railroad job reserved for whites only, and so on. Beyond these day-to-day events—through the instrumentality of Van Onselen's letters—we are privy to the aims of powerful politicians who respond to all opposition with increasingly harsh penalties. In his second letter, for example, Van Onselen informs his aunt that the penalty for inciting anyone to disobey even a trivial law by way of protest has been increased to five years in prison and ten lashes, and also that "any preaching of racial equality will in future be regarded as an attempt to further the aims of Communism." There are other letter-writers in this novel. Among them is the anonymous "Proud White Christian Woman" whose letters to opponents of apartheid are invariably obscene.

As always in Paton's writings, there are universal concerns behind the depiction of these instances of South African racial attitudes. In the first episode a social system proclaiming itself to be Christian responds ruthlessly to actions based on the Gandhian principle of nonviolent opposition, *satyagraha*. This point is underlined by an elderly Hindu who tells Prem Bodasingh, ". . . If you ever become a Christian, you must keep your eyes on Christ so that you will not get a chance to look at Christians." The second episode, "The Cleft Stick," presents variations on the question Paton explored in his biography of Jan Hofmeyr: should a person of conscience in a position of public trust resign in protest against unjust laws or seek to soften their effect through compassionate administration? Should one remain in South Africa and oppose apartheid or leave it for the sake of one's children? Robert Mansfield, who has private means, resigns his post as principal of a white school and joins the Liberal party to oppose apartheid. Later, in the face of violent vigilante attacks on his family, he emigrates to Australia to ensure their safety. His friend, the aging black headmaster Wilberforce Nhlapo, who cannot risk outspoken opposition, must endure the contempt of more youthful black militants.

In the fourth episode, "Death of a Traitor," Paton returns to the theme of the idolatry of pure race—"the sin against the blood"—that occupied him in *Too Late the Phalarope*. Here a high-ranking government official commits suicide after violating the prohibition against sexual contact across racial lines. The fifth episode, "The Holy Church of Zion," is a wonderfully ironic and comic satire on the Christian pretensions of the proponents of *apartheid*. At a place called Bochabela—near Bloemfontein (the seat of South Africa's supreme court)—a minister of the white Reformed Church strictly enforcing Dr. Hendrik's "church clause" of 1957 refuses to admit black mourners wishing to attend the funeral services of a respected white township official. A local black clergyman then asks a judge of the supreme court to join his congregation in a Good Friday service and take part in the ceremony of the washing of feet as a form of reconciliation. The judge agrees to wash the feet of a black woman—an old family retainer who has been nurse to all his children. During the ceremony he remembers how this woman used to kiss his children's feet after bathing them; and he kisses the feet he has just washed. By chance, a white newspaper reporter witnesses the scene and headlines it—to the horror of many white Christians including the Minister for Justice.

Ah, But Your Land Is Beautiful was very well received in South Africa by those who tended to share Paton's views, and particularly by those who had lived through the events it portrays. Reviewers elsewhere were impressed by Paton's ability to keep the story of such sombre circumstances so light and dramatic. Writing in *Newsweek*, 15 March 1982, Peter S. Prescott said: "The 28 years that have elapsed since Alan Paton last published a novel have in no way diminished—indeed, they seem to have strengthened—the skills which this South African writer brings to his fiction." In particular, Prescott found the awesome presence of Dr. Hendrik, "conveyed wholly through the praise of an admirer," to be "a technical marvel." Since the presence of Dr. Hendrik takes over more forcefully in the Epilogue, "Into the Golden Age," it forebodes an intensification of the exercise of the powers of intimidation and repression in the parts of the trilogy yet to come; and, in the face of this, it promises a new epiphany of the terrible beauty of human courage and human frailty. Paton's courage at undertaking such a task in his eightieth year is itself remarkable.

Notes and References

Chapter One

1. *Lost in the Stars*, a musical tragedy, with book by Maxwell Anderson; music by Kurt Weill; based on Alan Paton's novel *Cry, the Beloved Country*; staged by Rouben Mamoulian; presented by the Playwrights Company at the Music Box Theatre, New York. The play opened 30 October 1949 and continued for 273 performances. Revived as an opera by the New York City Opera Company during the 1950 spring season. Text: Maxwell Anderson, *Lost in the Stars* (New York, 1950), 86 pp.

2. *Cry, the Beloved Country*, London Films, 1951. Directed by Zoltan Korda. Filmed partly in South African settings. Canada Lee as Stephen Kumalo; Sidney Poitier as Absalom. United States distribution by Lopert. Rental: Audio Film Center, 2138 East 75th Street, Chicago.

3. *Cry, the Beloved Country: A Verse Drama*; adapted from Alan Paton's novel by Felicia Komai with the collaboration of Josephine Douglas. First produced in the church of St. Martin-in-the-Fields, London, February 1954. First published London: Edinburgh House, 1954, 80 pp.; New York: Friendship Press, 1955.

4. Translations of *Cry, the Beloved Country* soon appeared in many countries including Norway, Sweden, Denmark, The Netherlands, Finland, Czechoslovakia, France, Italy, Israel, Japan, Greece, Yugoslavia, Spain, and Portugal. In South Africa it was translated into Afrikaans and Zulu, in India into Hindi, and in Iran into Persian.

5. "Editorial," *Reality* 1 (March 1969):3. This editorial is unsigned, but Paton initialed Edward Callan's copy.

6. "Jan Hendrick Hofmeyr—An Appreciation," *South African Opinion*, 18 September 1936, pp. 6—7. ("Signed M. P. to give the impression of inside knowledge, but in fact the letters stood for Mr. Paton"—see *Hofmeyr*, p. 236 n.).

7. Alan Paton, "His Excellency the Governor," *Natal University College Magazine* 9 (October 1923):17—19.

8. Edward Callan, *Alan Paton*, TWAS 40 (New York, 1968), pp. 28—30.

9. Alan Paton, "Ladysmith," *Natal University College Magazine* 5 (November 1921):10—11.

10. Ibid. 7 (Winter term 1922):34—35.

11. Alan Paton, "The Imperial Conference," *Natal University College Magazine* 11 (October 1924):9—12. Source of all subsequent references to the conference.

12. That Ixopo High School served white students is emphasized here because many sources rely on misleading text and photographs in *Life* (November 1949), pp. 142—43, showing Paton with Zulu children at a small mission school at Ixopo "like the one . . . where he used to teach."

13. Alan Paton, "Tragic and Lovely Land of South Africa," *Holiday* 21 (February 1957):34.

14. Alan Paton, "The New Physics," *Natal University College Magazine*, Commemoration Number (1934):37—39.

Chapter Two

1. Letter to Edward Callan, April 1966.

2. Guy Butler, ed., *A Book of South African Verse* (London: Oxford University Press, 1959), p. 72.

3. Remarks by Mr. Alan Paton in "Minutes of a Conference on Urban Juvenile Native Delinquency Held at Johannesburg," October 1938, pp. 10—12. (From the files of the South African Institute of Race Relations.)

4. Alan Paton "Juvenile Delinquency and Its Treatment," *Community and Crime: Penal Reform Pamphlets, No. 3* (Pretoria: Van Schaik 1949), p. 53.

5. Alan Paton, *Hofmeyr* (Cape Town, 1964), p. 274; *South African Tragedy* (New York, 1965), p. 211.

6. Alan Paton, "Let's Build Model Prisons," *Forum* 7 (27 May 1944):24.

7. W.H. Auden, *The Dyer's Hand* (New York: Random House, 1962), p. 84.

8. Alan Paton, "The Real Way to Cure Crime," *Forum* 7 (29 January 1944):24.

9. Ibid.

10. Alan Paton, "A Deep Experience," in *The Long View* (New York, 1968), pp. 58—59.

11. Paton discusses this conference in *Towards the Mountain* (New York, 1980) pp. 259—61. He wrote an immediate account of it for the *Outspan* (South Africa) 40 (13 September 1946):34—35.

Chapter Three

1. Alan Paton, "Who Is Really to Blame . . . ," *Forum* 8 (15 December 1945):7—8; source of quotations in the three paragraphs following.

2. Horton Davies, "Alan Paton: Literary Artist and Anglican," *Hibbert Journal* 1 (April 1952):266.

3. Hoernlé's writings: R.F.A. Hoernlé, *South African Native Policy and the Liberal Spirit* (Cape Town: Cape Town University Press, 1939); *Race and Reason*, ed. with a memoir by J. D. MacCrone (Johannesburg: Witwatersrand University Press, 1945).

4. J. M. Synge, Preface to *The Playboy of the Western World* (Dublin: Maunsel, 1907); Alan Paton, interview with John K. Hutchens, *New York Herald Tribune Book Review*, 6 November 1949, p. 2.

5. Although Jarvis reads it, the Gettysburg Address is not quoted in the novel.

Chapter Four

1. Austin Roberts, *The Birds of South Africa* (6th ed., Johannesburg: Central News Agency, 1948); revised by A. McLaughlin and R. Liversidge (Johannesburg: Central News Agency, 1957). Phalarope: ploverlike or snipelike birds that "swim more than other waders and often seek their food far from land on the surface of the water" (Roberts, *The Birds of South Africa*, 5th ed., 1940).

2. L. C. Bekker and G. J. Potgieter, *Voorlighting vir Standerd VIII* (Johannesburg, 1960), p. 48 ff. Quotation translated by Edward Callan.

3. Alan Paton, "The South African Novel in English," *Knocking on the Door* (New York, 1975), p. 141.

4. Paton may have hit on the device of the diary after his own unexpected discovery of a personal diary among Jan Hofmeyr's papers—"But the big discovery was the diary . . . without this corroboration many people would have rejected the closing chapters of the biography"—"The Hofmeyr Biography," *Contrast* 10 (October 1964):33.

Chapter Five

1. Alan Paton, *Tales from a Troubled Land* (New York, 1961); *Debbie Go Home* (London, 1961). For dates of individual publications of these stories see the bibliography appended to the first edition of this TWAS study (1968).

2. Trevor Huddleston, *Naught for Your Comfort* (New York: Doubleday, 1956), p. 80.

3. Alan Paton, "A Personal View," *New York Times*, 29 March 1964, Sec. 2, p. 1.

4. Alan Paton, "The Prevention of Crime," *Race Relations* 12, no. 3 (1945):42.

5. *Spoионо* by Alan Paton and Krishna Shah. Staged by Krishna Shah. Presented by Mary K. Frank. Traditional chants arranged by Gideon Nxumalo. Presented at the Cort Theater, New York, for twenty performances: Thursday, 2 April 1964, to Saturday, 18 April 1964. Krishna Shah is best known in the United States for his direction of Tagore's *King of the Dark Chambers*, which ran for 255 performances.

6. Howard Taubman, review of *Spoионо, New York Times*, 3 April 1964, p. 28.

7. Gene Cole, review of *Spoионо, Intermission* 2 (6 March 1966):3. *Intermission Magazine* is published by Hull House Theater, Chicago, Illinois.

8. Taubman, review of *Spoионо*, p. 28.

9. Richard A. Duprey, "Play of the Month," *Catholic World* 199 (June 1964):199−200.

10. *Spoионо*, directed by Michael Miller, Parkway Community Theater, Chicago. Opened Friday, 25 February 1966, for ten weekends.

11. Richard Christiansen, review of *Spoионо, Chicago Daily News*, 28 February 1966, p. 32.

Chapter Six

1. Alan Paton, "The South African Novel in English," in *Knocking on the Door*, p. 142.

2. Alan Paton, "The Trial," *Contact* 9 (April 1966):7.

3. Alan Paton, "The Novelist and Christ" (with Liston Pope), *Saturday Review*, 4 December 1954, pp. 15−16.

4. Louis Nkosi, *Home and Exile* (London: Oxford University Press, 1965), p. 58.

5. Alan Paton, "Nationalism and the Theatre," in *The Long View*, pp. 256−57.

6. Letter to Edward Callan, August 1966.

7. See Callan, *Alan Paton* (TWAS, 1968), pp. 101−102.

Chapter Seven

1. Alan Paton, "Where Are You Going, Afrikaner?" *Sunday Tribune*, Durban, 13 May 1973; reprinted in *Knocking on the Door*, pp. 262−64. He names four distinguished Afrikaners who opposed *apartheid* and were therefore deemed "traitors" by the Afrikaner Nationalists in power: E. G. Malherbe, vice-chancellor and principal of the University of Natal who had headed the Army Education Service in World War II, of which Paton says in *Apartheid and the Archbishop* (Cape Town, 1973): "The members of the

Service challenged the racial laws, customs, and conventions of South Africa and opened the eyes of many to the inconsistency of fighting Hitler abroad and supporting segregation at home." Leo Marquard, founder of NUSAS (National Union of South African Students), historian (*The Peoples and Policies of South Africa* [London: Oxford University Press, 1952; rev. ed. 1960]), and second-in-command to Malherbe in the Army Education Service; Uys Krige, poet, playwright, and short-story writer, subject of *Uys Krige* (TWAS 2) by Christine van Heyningen and Jacques Berthoud; the Reverend Beyers Nandé, noted theologian of the Dutch Reformed Church and founder of the Christian Institute, which was banned by the South African government in 1980.

2. See, e.g., "List of Banned Liberals," in *The Long View*, Appendix A, pp. 277–78.

3. Quoted by Paton in *Hope for South Africa* (London, 1958), p. 27.

4. Albert Luthuli, *Let My People Go* (New York: McGraw Hill, 1962), p. 139.

5. Alan Paton, "Letter from Alan Paton," *Saturday Review*, 22 August 1952, p. 10.

6. Both articles appeared in *Colliers*, 134 (15 October 1954):20, 52–56; and 134 (29 October 1954):70–80.

7. John Gassner, "*Too Late the Phalarope*: Alternatives in Social Drama," in *Theatre at the Crossroads* (New York: Holt, Rinehart & Winston, 1960), pp. 177–80.

8. Mary Benson, *The African Patriots* (New York: Encyclopaedia Britannica Press, 1964), p. 274. For Paton's views on the Treason Trial and a more complete description of the Defence Fund, see his "On Trial for Treason," *New Republic* 137 (11 November 1957):9–12; and "South African Treason Trial," *Atlantic* 205 (January 1960):78–81.

9. Alan Paton in *The Long View*, p. 233.

10. Editorial comment, *Contact* 7 (August 1964):1.

11. Editorial comment, *Contact* 3 (27 August 1960):6.

12. Aaron Levenstein and William Agar, *Freedom's Advocate* (New York: Viking, 1965), p. 153. Also the source of quoted material in the next two paragraphs including remarks by President Eisenhower and Archibald MacLeish.

13. Alan Paton in *The Long View*, p. 168.

14. Alan Paton, *Contact* 3 (17 December 1960):2.

Chapter Eight

1. Alan Paton, "Jan Hendrik Hofmeyr: An Appreciation," *South African Opinion*, 18 September 1936, pp. 7, 12. "It was signed M. P. to give the

impression of inside knowledge, but in fact the letters stood for Mr. Paton"
(Paton, *Hofmeyr*, 236). This is not the journal *South African Opinion* published
during 1944—1947, but an earlier journal of the same name.

2. Alan Paton, "The Hofmeyr Biography," *Contrast* 3 (October 1965):
32—36.

3. William Plomer, Preface to *The Little Karoo* by Pauline Smith
(London: Cape, 1950).

4. Extract quoted in Horton Davies, "Alan Paton: Literary Artist and
Anglican," *Hibbert Journal* 1 (April 1952):263.

5. Paton, "The Hofmeyr Biography" (note 2, above), source of quotation in preceding paragraph.

6. Alan Paton, "South African Story," *Times Literary Supplement*, 29
April 1965, p. 328.

7. Paton, "The Hofmeyr Biography" (note 2, above).

8. Jan Hofmeyr, in *Forum* 1 (26 September 1938). Quoted in *Hofmeyr*,
pp. 294—95.

9. Quoted from Tom MacDonald, *Jan Hofmeyr: Heir to Smuts* (London:
1948), pp. 12—13. Paton discusses this speech in *Hofmeyr*, pp. 421—23;
South African Tragedy, pp. 325—27.

10. Alan Paton, interview with Studs Terkel, *Perspective on Ideas and the
Arts* (Gale Broadcasting Company, Chicago) 12 (May 1963):29. Quoted by
permission of Studs Terkel.

11. Ibid.

12. Paton, "The Hofmeyr Biography," p. 33.

Chapter Nine

1. Aleksandr Solzhenitsyn, *The Gulag Archipelago, 1918—1956*, tr.
Thomas P. Whitney (New York: Harper, 1973), p. 174.

2. Edward B. Fiske, "Witness against Apartheid" (review of *Apartheid
and the Archbishop* by Alan Paton), *New York Times*, 10 May 1976, p. 35.

3. Robert F. Capon, review of *Instrument of Thy Peace*; *New York Times
Book Review*, 24 March 1968, p. 12.

Chapter Ten

1. Auden, *The Dyer's Hand*, p. 85.

2. Thomas Pakenham, review of *Towards the Mountain*, *New York Times
Book Review*, 12 October 1981, p. 8.

3. Tony Voss, "Getting Up There Again," *Reality* 7 (January 1976): 17—19.

4. John S. Dunne, *A Search for God in Time and Memory* (Notre Dame,
Ind.: University of Notre Dame Press, 1977), p. 47.

Selected Bibliography

PRIMARY SOURCES

1. Novels

Ah, But Your Land Is Beautiful. New York: Charles Scribner's Sons, 1981. The first novel of a projected trilogy set against the background of the Liberal party period, 1953–68.

Cry, the Beloved Country. New York: Charles Scribner's Sons, 1948. Dedication: "To Aubrey and Marigold Burns of Fairfax, California." Chapters numbered continuously throughout. Reissued: Scribner's Modern Standard Authors, with Author's Note and introduction by Lewis Gannett, 1950.

Cry, the Beloved Country: A Story of Comfort in Desolation. London: Jonathan Cape, 1948. Dedication: "To my wife and to my friend of many years Jan Hendrik Hofmeyr." Chapters numbered within books One, Two, and Three.

Too Late the Phalarope. Cape Town: Cannon (for Jonathan Cape), 1953; New York: Charles Scribner's Sons, 1953.

2. Short Stories

Debbie Go Home. London: Jonathan Cape, 1961. Published in New York as *Tales from a Troubled Land*. See listing below.

Tales from a Troubled Land. New York: Charles Scribner's Sons, 1961. The same ten short stories as *Debbie Go Home* differently arranged.

3. Plays

Lost in the Stars (with Maxwell Anderson). New York: Sloane Associates, 1950.

Mkhumbane [Village in the Gulley]. Libretto for a musical by Todd Matshikiza, performed at Durban City Hall, March 21–27, 1960. Not published.

Sponono (with Krishna Shah). New York: Charles Scribner's Sons, 1965. A three-act play based on stories from *Tales from a Troubled Land*.

Too Late the Phalarope. A drama by Robert Yale Libott from the novel by Alan
    Paton. Presented by Mark K. Frank at the Belasco Theatre, New York,
    11 October 1965. Not published.

4. Biography

*Apartheid and the Archbishop: The Life and Times of Geoffrey Clayton. Archbishop
    of Cape Town*. Cape Town: David Philip, 1973; New York: Charles
    Scribner's Sons, 1973.
Hofmeyr. Cape Town: Oxford University Press, 1964. Published in the
    United States as *South African Tragedy*. See following listing.
South African Tragedy: The Life and Times of Jan Hofmeyr. Abridgment by
    Dudley C. Lunt; prefatory note, vii—x; editorial note, pp. 413—15.
    New York: Charles Scribner's Sons, 1965.

5. Autobiographies

For You Departed. New York: Charles Scribner's Sons, 1969. Published in
    London as *Kontakion for You Departed*. London: Jonathan Cape, 1969.
Towards the Mountain. New York: Charles Scribner's Sons, 1980; London:
    Jonathan Cape, 1981.

6. Essays: History, Politics, Religion

"Americans and Us." *Reality*, September 1977, pp. 6—7. His reasons for
    seeing the United States Secretary of State, Cyrus Vance.
"Challenge of Fear." In *What I Have Learned: A Collection of Twenty Auto-
    biographical Essays from the "Saturday Review."* New York: Simon and
    Schuster, 1968, pp. 250—60.
Charlestown Story. Pietermaritzburg: Liberal Party Publications, 1960.
    Pamphlet explaining the effects of the Group Areas Act on Africans
    removed from freehold land. Excerpt reprinted in *The Long View*.
Christian Unity: A South African View. Peter Ainslie Memorial Lecture.
    Grahamstown: Rhodes University, 1951.
D.C.S. Oosthuizen Memorial Lectures, Number One. Grahamstown: Rhodes
    University Academic Freedom Committee, 1970. Contains Paton's
    poem in memory of four students killed at Kent State University.
Hope for South Africa. London: Pall Mall, 1958; New York: Praeger, 1959.
Instrument of Thy Peace. New York: The Seabury Press, 1968. A book of
    Lenten meditations.

Land and People of South Africa. Portraits of the Nations Series. Philadelphia: Lippincott, 1955, rev. ed. 1974. Published in Britain as *South Africa and Her People*. London: Lutterworth, 1957.

"Lutuli Memorial Service." *Reality*, September 1972, pp. 3−4.

People Wept: Being a Brief Account of the Origin, Contents, and Application of that Unjust Law of the Union of South Africa Known as the Group Areas Act of 1950 (Since Consolidated as Act. No. 77 of 1957). Kloof, Natal: Alan Paton, 1958. Excerpt reprinted in *The Long View*.

"Roy Campbell." In *Aspects of South African Literature*. Edited by Christopher Heywood. London: Heinemann; New York: Africana Publishing Company, 1976, pp. 3−23.

South Africa in Transition (with Dan Weiner). Text by Alan Paton and photographs by Dan Weiner. New York: Charles Scribner's Sons, 1956.

South Africa Today. Public Affairs Pamphlet No. 175. New York: Public Affairs Committee, 1951; London: Lutterworth Press, 1953.

"Why Suffering?" In *Creative Suffering: The Ripple of Hope*. Kansas City: National Catholic Reporter* and the Pilgrim Press, 1970, pp. 13−22.

7. Collected Writings

Knocking on the Door: Shorter Writings of Alan Paton. Edited by Colin Gardner. New York: Charles Scribner's Sons, 1975.

The Long View. Edited by Edward Callan with a Foreword by Alan Paton. New York: Praeger, 1968; London: Pall Mall, 1968; Stockholm: Nordsets, 1969. A selection of Paton's "Long View" essays from *Contact*, his Freedom Award speech (1960), and "A Deep Experience."

SECONDARY SOURCES

1. Bibliographies

Bentel, Lea. *Alan Paton: A Bibliography*. Johannesburg: University of the Witwatersrand Department of Bibliography, Librarianship and Typography, 1969.

Callan, Edward. "Selected Bibliography." In *Alan Paton*. TWAS 40, 1st ed. New York: Twayne, 1968. Contains "Juvenalia" and other material not in Bentel.

————, ed. *Alan Paton*. Hamburger Bibliographien, Band 11. Translated by F. Weidner; compiled by Rolf Italiaander. Hamburg: Hans Christians Verlag, 1970. In German; the most complete listing to date.

2. Articles and Parts of Books

Breit, Harvey. *The Writer Observed*. New York: World, 1956. Contains an interview with Alan Paton.

Davies, Horton. *A Minor for the Ministry in Modern Novels*, New York: Oxford University Press, 1959. Gives an analysis of *Cry, the Beloved Country*.

Fuller, Edmund. *Books with the Man Behind Them*. New York: Random House, 1962. Contains an evaluation of Paton's novels.

Gardiner, Harold. *In All Conscience*. New York: Hanover House, 1959. Reprints Gardiner's reviews in *America* of *Cry, the Beloved Country* and *Too Late the Phalarope*.

Italiaander, Rolf, " 'Auf die Docher!' Alan Paton, der Streitbare Christ." In *Alan Paton*. Hamburger Bibliographien, Band 11. Hamburg: Hans Christians Verlag, 1970, pp. 5-16. In German.

Prescott, Orville. *In My Opinion*. New York: Bobbs-Merrill, 1952. Selects *Cry, the Beloved Country* as one of the four great novels of recent years.

Rooney, Charles. "The Message of Alan Paton." *Catholic World*, November 1961, pp. 92–98. An analysis of Paton's fiction.

Voss, Tony. "Getting Up There Again: A Review of Alan Paton's *Knocking on the Door*." *Reality*, January 1976, pp. 17–19.

Wästberg, Per. "Alan Paton: Rösten Inifran Muråna." In Paton, Alan. *På Lång Sikt*. Stockholm: Norsteds, 1969. Introduction to Swedish edition of *The Long View*.

Index

DATE DUE
